Australian Biographical Monographs

14

Australian Biographical Monographs

Series Editor: Scott Prasser

Previous Volumes

Margaret Guilfoyle	Anne Henderson
William McKell	David Clune
Neville Bonner	Sean Jacobs
George Reid	Luke Wallker
Robert Askin	Paul Loughnan
John Grey Gorton	Paul Williams
Stanley Melbourne Bruce	David Lee
Robert Menzies	Scott Prasser
Neville Wran	David Clune
Lindsay Thompson	William Westerman
Johannes Bjelke-Petersen	Bruce Kingston
Harold Holt	Tom Frame
Joseph Lyons	Kevin Andrews

Australian Biographical Monographs

14

Leonie Kramer

Damien Freeman

Connor Court Publishing

Australian Biographical Monographs 14
Leonie Kramer by Damien Freeman
Published in 2022 by Connor Court Publishing Pty Ltd

Copyright © Damien Freeman 2022

All rights reserved. No part of this book may be reproduced or transmitted in any form or by any means, electronic or mechanical, including photo copying, recording or by any information storage and retrieval system, without prior permission in writing from the publisher.

Connor Court Publishing Pty Ltd
PO Box 7257
Redland Bay QLD 4165
sales@connorcourt.com
www.connorcourt.com
Phone 0497-900-685

Printed in Australia

ISBN: 9781922449917

Cover image: the author, the dame and the prime minister at Kirribilli House, 18 November 1999.
Photo credit: the Honourable Natasha Maclaren-Jones MLC

to Zadie and Naomi Cahill
may you draw inspiration from the life of this great dame

Series overview

Connor Court's *Australian Biographical Monographs* series on past leading Australian political leaders and other important figures seeks to provide an overview for those who are unfamiliar with the subject and to highlight the person's particular importance, controversies, and contributions to Australia's progress.

The monographs are scholarly rather than academic in focus, placing emphasis on a clear narrative, but with careful attention to referencing to ensure views expressed are supported by appropriate sources and evidence.

The series was initiated because of the decline in the study of Australian history at our schools and universities. Consequently, there has been a lack of knowledge or, even worse, distorted views, of some of Australia's leading historical figures who deserve to be remembered, better understood for their achievements, and, as each volume also highlights, their flaws.

This monograph on Dame Leonie Kramer is the first in the series that is not on a former politician and so brings a refreshing look at another Australian who made important contributions to our education and cultural heritage. Indeed, in some ways, her contributions were more important than many of our elected officials. Nevertheless, Dame Leonie Kramer was very much in the public arena and not without controversy either expounding her views on her own specialty of literary criticism, debating her views on education or explaining and defending in open robust discussions with sometimes disgruntled politicians, ABC programs in her role as its Chairman. The monograph as its author admits is "neither a biography . . . nor a comprehensive assessment of her scholarship", but it is a valuable and informative insight of a significant and formable figure about whom we all should know more. Thanks to Damien Freeman – we now do.

-- Scott Prasser (Editor, *Australian Biographical Monographs*)

1
Leftovers

WELL OVER A decade before Lady Flo's pumpkin scones came to prominence, Dame Leonie's casserole recipe had already been published in the *Australian Women's Weekly*. First, pound dry flour into both sides of thick pieces of round steak; then fry lightly. Put the slices into a casserole dish with chopped onion, green peppers, and stuffed olives. Then pour one tin of concentrated tomato soup on top (no water), and put into the oven. Serve with whole olives.

The recipe may have been based on something she learnt in 1942 when undertaking studies for the Diploma in Domestic Economy presented to her by the somewhat confused wife of the Governor of Victoria, who assured her and the other women embarking on their undergraduate studies at the University of Melbourne that knowledge of the domestic arts would prove useful "when you return to civilian life."

Of the recipe's provenance little is known other than that it was published on 2 September 1959 in an article under the headline, WOMEN BORE MEN, in which "Mrs Kramer" is quoted as saying, "I blame Australian women entirely for the social segregation of the sexes and for allowing it to continue. It is time they became women of the twentieth century, cultivated some reasonably intelligent interest in life around them, in problems of the day; time they read more, argued more, and got away from the endless chatter about babies, shopping, clothes, and gossip." The *Women's Weekly* reassured readers that although she had a "formidable scholastic background," Mrs Kramer was no bluestocking: "she is a mother of two, expert housewife and cook, interested in clothes, charming to look at, delightful to talk to, completely feminine."

Mrs Kramer explained, "I've always loved teaching and lecturing but with husband, children and home, I have no ambition to aim at a professorship, to make a fulltime career of it. I'd much prefer to concentrate on cooking, for one of the really worthwhile things in life is to be a good cook." Yet she is introduced to readers by the *Women's Weekly*'s Ronald McKie with the words: "Tune into 'The Critics' on the ABC one of these Sunday evenings and you'll hear a slim, soft-voiced young woman quietly dominating, by her intellectual ability, the male members of the panel..."

For a woman of her generation, she achieved much that would have seemed beyond the ken of a woman a generation earlier, whilst at the same time managing to demonstrate the feminine virtues expected of that generation. This balancing act was managed at every point along the many steps of the steep ascent to the lofty heights that her career encompassed. She was the first woman to step foot in venerable domains that had hitherto been exclusively male. The determination that drove this ascent was evident in equal measure in her denunciation of feminism.

Much of her objection to feminism stems from the connections she saw between feminists and power. She believed that their ideology was an elaborate grab for power, both of which she claimed to reject. For all of that, it was noted in a profile piece in *The Bulletin* of 24 April 1979 that she had been phenomenally successful in accruing power for herself: "In appearance she typifies the attractive, well-groomed, intelligent and conservative women who are occasionally found among the more exclusive suburbs of Sydney and Melbourne," but she "is more than that—more intelligent, more hard-working, more experienced, more dedicated, more complex, and more interesting. Most important of all, she is more powerful." It continues to explain that through her involvement in official and private bodies, her "presence is pervasive, though not always identified, in Australian public life." In this way, she achieved a position from which "she helps mould the moulders of public opinion." Two decades after the *Women's Weekly* profile emphasised how she had succeeded in blending femininity and academic achievement, *The Bulletin* emphasises her power and the feminists' antipathy: "Distinguished from all but a handful of Australian women by her access to, and use of, power, Dr Kramer is no darling of the feminists." She claimed ignorance of such matters: "I don't think I've got any concept of power for myself. In fact, when I first became head of the department I used to joke with myself and look in the mirror to see if I felt that glorious sense of power, and nothing happened." Certainly, after half a century in public life, she was seen as a power player, particularly in conservative politics, notwithstanding the fact that she claimed to eschew power in Craig McGregor's 1990 book, *Headliners*, saying, "I don't like the exercise of power. I found that when you are at the top of the hierarchy what you acquire is enormous responsibility, but your capacity to exercise power is absolutely limited. Australians are obsessed with power."

By the end of her career, she was closely associated with the politics of John Howard, although she maintained she was not a party-political person and sought to maintain some kind of distance from the Liberal Party of Australia, resisting suggestions that she should be a Liberal Party senator; even refusing to be a member of the party. She was assuredly anti-communist in her thinking; however, this became a less meaningful stance after the end of the Cold War. Although she was variously characterized as a reactionary or a traditionalist, her aversion to communism and other ill-starred proposals for reform came from her innate conservatism. She was, at her core, a conservative in the mould of the eighteenth-century politician and philosopher, Edmund Burke. In *Reflections on the Revolution in France*, Burke condemns the French Revolution not because it involved change, but because of the *kind* of change it involved. It was abrupt and radical change based on theorising and abstract ideas, rather than gradual and modest change that was in keeping with the practical experience embodied by the country's tradition. Kramer believed in tradition in the sense that Burke did—as a guide to change. She was not opposed to change or progress, and would have concurred with Benjamin Disraeli, the nineteenth-century British prime minister, that "In a progressive country, change is constant and the great question is not whether you should resist change which is inevitable but whether change should be carried out in deference to the manners, the customs, the laws and the traditions of a people or whether it should be carried out in deference to abstract principles and arbitrary and general doctrines."

The tradition and its values was also central to her approach to Australian literature. This meant that her literary criticism was often at odds with contemporaries who took a rather different approach. Where she valued literature that demonstrated the development of the literary tradition through cultivation of personal style; they, perhaps, valued other things such as the cultivation of a national identity or social and political critique. Ultimately, her most notorious contretemps was with an author who fitted comfortably within her tradition, and who won the 1973 Nobel Prize for Literature for "an epic and psychological narrative art which has introduced a new continent into literature": Patrick White.

It was White who took to referring to her as Killer Kramer or simply The Kramer in private. White was a notorious hater, and so his private fulminations against her, on account of both her criticism of his novels and her politics, are unremarkable. He took this hatred to a new level with a wholly gratuitous and unambiguously indecorous reference to her in his autobiography, *Flaws in the Glass*. What is remarkable, however, is the way in which her criticism of White's novels allowed her to home in on concerns that were some of her own deepest preoccupations.

When interviewing her in preparation for his pen portrait, McGregor was struck by the way that Kramer talked about White. At one point, she declared him to be "at heart a real sceptic." Then some days later she told McGregor, "I'm a sceptic." The parallels became more astonishing to McGregor, particularly when Kramer tried to articulate her "great respect for religious belief" by reference to White. She told McGregor:

> "I don't know what I am. I'm certainly not an atheist; an agnostic is a silly thing to be. I'm a leftover. Patrick keeps raising . . . he keeps grappling with

> this... what happens if God is dead? It's the question Dostoevsky asked. What are the sanctions? It's very important for people to recognise they didn't make the world, man is not the measure of all things, there is something beyond... You have to hold on to the belief that God isn't dead in order to provide that dimension which is non-material..."

McGregor explains that he slowly realised that "though she was explicating Patrick White's position, she was in fact talking about herself." And it happens again when she talks about White's "intellectual snobbery" and his "apparent condemnation of the common people—I won't wear that." McGregor sees this in White's commitment to populist causes from which Kramer seems to him to have "kept herself aloof." His conclusion: "It's as though White represents some alternative persona, some illicit strain in herself which she recognises but rejects. They are both aristocrats in a common-place; it is not themselves but their reactions which differ."

What follows is a sketch of Kramer's life which emphasises those aspects that she regarded as important for her development. From there, we consider two subjects central to her professional life: first, her approach to the nature of education, teaching, and universities; secondly, her approach to Australian literature. Finally, we consider Kramer's attitude to culture, society, and the state, and how this informed her contribution to public life. What emerges is one coherent theme that is a current moving through each of the tributaries that flow into the river of her life: a radical-conservative approach to tradition and change.

In the end, this is a book about Kramer as a public figure—not a scholar or intellectual. It was commissioned by Connor Court Publishing as part of its Australian Biographical Monographs series. Those profiled in the series include Joseph Lyons, Harold Holt, Sir Robert Menzies, Sir Joh Bjelke-Petersen, Sir John Gorton, Sir Robert Askin, and Viscount Bruce of Melbourne. They are all statesmen; she was not. She played more than a bit part, however, in public life for well over half a century. This book seeks to demonstrate that Burke's worldview underpinned both Kramer's scholarly and public lives.

In the end, Dame Leonie might have regarded herself as a leftover, but her contribution to public life and the worldview that informed it was every bit as rich as her casserole.

2
Lioness

LEONIE, MEANING 'LIONESS', is the feminine form of a given name that can be traced back to Leo, the Latin for 'lion'. In this case, the choice of name seems to have been a portent for the life of Leonie Judith Gibson.

Leonie was born to Gertrude Isabel (née Walker), known as Judy, and Alfred Leonard Gibson on 1 October 1924 in Melbourne. Judy and Alfred were married in 1909. He was born in Ballarat and entered the State Savings Bank of Victoria as a junior teller when he left school at the age of fourteen and rose to become the bank's publicity officer and a lay preacher for the Church of Christ. She was born in the Melbourne suburb of Preston and had aspirations for a medical career, which her father deemed unsuitable for a woman, so she instead studied piano and violin at the Albert Street Conservatorium. Both came from families that had migrated from England in the mid-nineteenth century. Together, they established a comfortable lower-middle-class home in Kew, where they cultivated their shared interests in learning and literature, in particular poetry and theatre. In their daughter's words, "They had inherited the traditions of the nineteenth century." Leonie was the second and last child of the marriage, the first being a son, Hartley, who was ten years old when his sister was born. Her schooling occurred at Presbyterian Ladies' College, Melbourne. In her last year at school, she won three scholarships which enabled her to continue her education at university.

Her recollections of childhood in the Gibson family home are of an ordered and stable existence in which the memory of the First World War cast a shadow and the Great Depression imposed austerity on the household and charity towards those less fortunate.

"Neither words nor displays of emotions were her ways of expressing feelings," Leonie later wrote of her mother. Rather, she remembered her mother reciting poetry to her every night long before she could read and introducing her to concert-going at a very early age. It was a time when an enduring desire to listen to music was awakened in her, as was an attachment to reading and theatre-going, as well as looking at pictures. They are memories couched in the language of action rather than passive appreciation.

She spent time with her father on local excursions to locations such as the wharves, where they would discuss the foreign places whence cargoes had arrived. She later recalled, "One day, he said, I would go to some of those places. So I grew up with a sense that there was a world to be explored outside my familiar one." Aside from these private conversations, her father's style of public speaking also seems to have had an enduring influence on her formidable approach to public speaking. In his preaching, she writes, "He interpreted Biblical texts in a way which everyone could understand, and related them to common human experiences. His sceptical mind was not given to rhetorical flourishes (which he liked to parody) or to large pronouncements." The early experience of his preaching was consolidated by the Presbyterian principles of her schooling, which she found "both demanding and tolerant." Aside from worship, social work was an important feature of the school's ethos, and Leonie was required to take two children from the local orphanage to the zoo each weekend and pay for them out of her pocket money: "We learnt how to care about them and help them without being patronising. Faith and works were inseparable."

To the University

In 1942, she moved into Janet Clarke Hall, the sister college to Trinity College at the University of Melbourne. She had initially intended to study modern languages, having thought that she might become a secretary to a consul and travel the world with him, but ended up studying German, French, English, and philosophy in her first year, and continued on to take combined Honours in the latter two, graduating as a Bachelor of Arts with combined First Class Honours in 1945. Her university years overlapped with the latter part of the Second World War and this profoundly coloured her experience.

She studied aesthetics with the Professor of Philosophy, Alexander (Sandy) Boyce Gibson, who would also help her on her way to Oxford, but perhaps the dominant influence in her undergraduate years was George Paul, a philosopher who had been at St Andrews and Cambridge, and who was responsible for introducing the philosophy of Wittgenstein to Melbourne, before departing for Oxford in 1945. His analysis of early Greek philosophy left a deep mark on the impressionably Leonie, who writes, "He discovered for us new ways of thinking, and my understanding of literature and especially poetry benefited greatly from his insights." In her final year, she attended a special subject for the three or four students doing joint Honours in philosophy and English. It was a study of philosophy, poetry, fiction, and criticism at the time of the mid-eighteenth-century transition from the Augustan Age to the Romantic Age. It was to this course that she attributed her "life-long interest in the shift of mood and attitudes in literary history." It was also an opportunity to study intensively the poetry of Matthew Arnold, in which she took a special interest. Arnold would become a major influence on her approach to literary criticism, but she also attributed to his two Oxford poems, 'Thyrsis' and 'The Scholar Gypsy', her "romantic dream of the unknown" Oxford's dreaming spires.

It was wartime, however, and so formal studies also had to make way for extracurricular activities including first-aid classes, digging trenches, learning how to extinguish incendiary bombs, and making blackout curtains. Her memory of the day the war in the Pacific ended remained one of her most vivid memories into old age: "George Paul invited his small group of Honours students to his home. We sat around him celebrating, while he, semi-reclining on a couch, read to us from *The Iliad*. None of us had Greek, but we were all mesmerised by the sound of the language, and his summary at the beginning was sufficient to make us feel that we understood."

The year 1945 was a decisive one in her life, not only because the war ended and she graduated, but also because her father died suddenly that year, leaving her to support her mother emotionally and practically (amongst other things, she assumed responsibility for mowing the lawn). All along, she had had her sights set on Oxford and her undergraduate studies had only strengthened the desire to go there. In the meantime, she accepted a tutorship in

English from the rector of Newman College, a residential college within the university, and a junior tutorship in the English Department at the university, as well as marking papers for the Leaving Certificate. She began working on a research thesis on the twentieth-century Irish poet, William Butler Yeats, for a Master of Arts degree, but swiftly swapped to write on the Australian female novelist, Henry Handel Richardson, when the opportunity arose for her to study newly available Richardson manuscripts sent to the National Library of Australia after Richardson's death in 1946. This research became the basis for her first book, *Henry Handel Richardson and Some of Her Sources*.

It is notable that A. D. Hope, who later became a celebrated poet about whom Leonie would write, was a frequent visitor to her mother's home; one upon whose friendship her mother placed great store. It is a reminder that, although her family home was socially humble, it was culturally rich. In later life, detractors would claim that she had the sort of upper-class background that Patrick White did. In fact, her family home was relatively modest. What marked it out was the depth of cultural attainment achieved despite this.

As it happened, the registrar of the University of Oxford visited the University of Melbourne at this time, with a view to establishing a system of exchange between doctoral students at the two universities. With the encouragement of Boyce Gibson, she saw the opportunity this provided to realize her dream of going to Oxford. She applied to be an exchange student and was successful. The registrar, who was also chairman of the council of St Hugh's College, Oxford, then had a hand in arranging an affiliation for her with St Hugh's and, with the aid of a British Council travel grant, she set sail for London in 1949.

Oxford

Leonie Gibson left Australia in 1949 and Leonie Kramer returned in 1953. These four years were, without doubt, the defining ones of her life. Their significance became apparent when her memoirs were published in 2012. The first twenty-five years of her life are recounted in three chapters. In contrast, seven chapters are devoted to the next four years. The remaining eleven chapters deal with almost half a century of her life, up until her forced resignation as Chancellor of the University of Sydney in 2001, when the memoir gives the impression that her life's story ended.

She took ship on the *Otranto* at Melbourne in late August 1949 and voyaged for five weeks, first to Fremantle, then across the Indian Ocean to Colombo, and on through the Red Sea and the Suez Canal, into the Mediterranean, where she celebrated her twenty-fifth birthday in the Bay of Biscay, thence through the Straits of Gibraltar to the white cliffs of Dover and up the Thames to London where she stayed for three nights, before making her way to Oxford.

During the summer of 1949, Leonie made a daytrip on the back of a motorbike to view an archaeological site in St Albans, and afterwards returned to Halifax House, the graduate students' club in Oxford, where she met Harold Kramer for the first time. Harry was studying for the degree of Doctor of Philosophy in pathology under the Regius Professor of Pathology, Alistair Robb-Smith. He was born in Cape Town in 1918 and graduated from the University of Cape Town in medicine in 1940, before serving as a captain in the South African Medical Corps in Africa, the Middle East, and Italy for six years, then returning to Cape Town to pursue an academic career in pathology and bacteriology. After participating in a scientific expedition to Tristan da Cunha in 1948, he proceeded to Oxford later that year as Nuffield Dominions Demonstrator in Pathology. He married Leonie in 1952 and they were both awarded the DPhil at the same ceremony in 1953.

The places she experienced during these defining years had a lasting impact on her, and this was no less true of Oxford than of those visited on a seven-week trip to Europe in 1950 (starting in Paris and thence Versailles, Chartres, Cannes, Nice, Monte Carlo, Milan, Venice, Bologna, Verona, the Dolomites, to Austria for the Salzburg Festival, the Oberammergau Passion Play, and the Vienna Philharmonic Orchestra) and another to Ireland (by ferry from Liverpool to Dublin, and then by train to Killarney) for Christmas that year. She returned to France in 1951, where she and Harry travelled 1,500 miles on motorbike. Harry also took her on a trip to Rome, which he wanted to show her, as he had been posted there with the occupying forces for fifteen months after the defeat of Mussolini.

In Oxford, aside from settling into reading and tutorials for her BLitt (Bachelor of Letters—a second undergraduate degree), there were all sorts of lectures to attend, plenty of extra-curricular activities organised by the Archaeological Society and the Bach Choir, and excursions into the countryside, as well as to London and

Cambridge. Towards the end of her life, she concluded that it was the incidental things, rather than the formal research activities, that had been the decisive aspect of her time in Oxford. It was in the people she met along the way; the conversations she had; the places she visited—more than what she learnt in the lecture hall or the library—that it seemed to her that the enduring value of Oxford was to be found.

She decided to transfer from the BLitt to the DPhil, allegedly because she realised that if her DPhil thesis didn't merit that degree, she would be awarded the BLitt. Her DPhil thesis was on formal satire in England from 1590 to 1650. Satire served an important political purpose during this period, in that it was a vehicle for political commentary that would otherwise be forbidden, however, it often lacked literary merit. Ever pragmatic, Kramer maintained that the study of bad verse was an excellent training for a career in literary criticism.

She was obliged to return to Melbourne in 1952 to give a course of lectures on non-fictional prose in the nineteenth century before returning to Oxford to graduate. Harry had no desire to return to apartheid South Africa. Thus, when he obtained a position at the newly established Australian National University, they set up home in Australia on a permanent basis.

Canberra and Sydney

In 1953, the Kramers left Oxford and set sail for Melbourne via Cape Town. Leonie had given birth to her first daughter, Jocelyn, and this trip was an opportunity for Harry's family to meet his wife and daughter. Then to Melbourne where Harry met Leonie's brother, but not her mother, who had died shortly before they were able to visit her. Then on to Canberra, where Howard Florey had offered Harry a position in the Department of Pathology at the new John Curtin School, and where Leonie obtained some lecturing work at Canberra University College.

When their second daughter, Hilary, was born in Canberra, the Kramer family was complete. Harry obtained a position as senior pathologist at the New South Wales State Cancer Council Special Unit, and the family moved to Sydney in 1956, when Jocelyn was three and Hilary two. They purchased a house in Vaucluse, and Leonie settled into keeping house. The years 1956 to 1958 were important ones in Kramer's development. Although she did not have an academic appointment at this time, she was nevertheless engaged actively in intellectual life. In particular, she joined the editorial board of *Quadrant* magazine when it was founded, and through that came in contact with a range of influential barristers, academics, businessmen, trade unionists, and journalists. She also wrote book reviews for *The Bulletin*, *Sydney Morning Herald*, *The Observer*, and *Nation*, as well as beginning her involvement with the ABC.

Whilst in Canberra, she had applied for a lectureship at the University of Sydney but received no reply to her application. In 1958, after more than a decade of teaching and studying, Kramer was appointed to her first fulltime tenured position as lecturer in the School of Humanities at the New South Wales University of Technology, soon to become the University of New South Wales. She was promoted to senior lecturer and then to associate professor (on her second attempt). Before the establishment of a faculty of arts, Kramer's students were drawn from faculties of applied science, wool technology, engineering, architecture, and other technical disciplines. They were required to study language and literature as part of their general studies. They were not necessarily interested in studying English, but Kramer enjoyed the challenge of coaxing them into reading in the hope that they might find interest and pleasure in it, rather than merely a burden. Many did not take to it, however, and it is important that this early experience of teaching was the experience of teaching reluctant conscripts rather than those who felt passionate about what they were studying.

In 1962, Kramer's contemporary, G. A. Wilkes, was named as the foundation Chair of Australian Literature at the University of Sydney. In 1966, he was appointed to the more prestigious Challis Chair of English Literature. Kramer applied for the Chair of Australian Literature and was appointed to it in 1968. She writes of this appointment in her memoirs, "When I applied for the Chair, I had little confidence in the outcome because my teaching experience in Australia Literature was limited, as was my research, which by today's standards seems rather thin. To my surprise, however, I was appointed in 1968. As it happened, I unwittingly created two records. I was the first woman Professor in the University of Sydney's history, and the last Professor to be appointed without interview. The new Vice-Chancellor, Professor Bruce Williams, had not yet had time to reform the selection procedures, which were little more than informal chats between interested parties. Later, I learnt that several people, including James McAuley and Alec Hope, had been invited to take the Chair, but they had declined, and I was cautioned by them against considering the position in the unlikely event that I would be offered it." She would hold the Chair until she retired in 1989.

As head of the English Department at Sydney University, she displayed her credentials as a radical conservative. She brought about changes that it seemed to her colleagues could not have been achieved by anyone else. For instance, she introduced provision for studying Australian literature without having previously taken an introductory course in English literature. This seemed very radical at the time, and it would have seemed too radical for anyone else to have proposed. She was also very pragmatic. In 1978, she accepted nine students from China who wished to study English in Australia as part of an arrangement that the Australian Government made to enable students to study in Australia for the first time after the Cultural Revolution. This presented administrative difficulties, but she contrived a means by which they could be enrolled for the MA degree on a 'probationary' basis, even though no such status existed. They were there, no doubt, to improve their language skills, but she introduced them to Australian literature with great success, and tailored courses to their needs without compromising standards in the examination processes.

Public life and Harvard

It was during this period that she began to take an active role in public life and civil society. To give a sense of her activities during this period, she was appointed a member of both the Corrective Services Advisory Council and the National Literature Board of Review in 1971 (the latter of which advised the Commonwealth Government in relation to censorship, until Lionel Murphy abolished it in 1972). In 1977, she was appointed commissioner of the Australian Broadcasting Commission, a position that she retained until it was replaced by the Australian Broadcasting Corporation in 1983. In 1984, she was appointed as a member of the Miles Franklin Literary Prize Committee, on which she served until 1997. Her service throughout this period was recognised in numerous ways including her appointment as an Officer of the Most Excellent Order of the British Empire in 1976. In 1983, she was advanced to Dame Commander of the Order for services to literature and the public.

The early 1980s were perhaps the highpoint of her professional career. In 1981, she published the *Oxford History of Australian Literature* before taking up her appointment as Visiting Professor in Australian Studies at Harvard University for 1981-82. She returned to Australia to serve as Chairman of the Australian Broadcasting Commission from 1982 until 1983, when it was reinvented as the Australian Broadcasting Corporation with a new board. Her career trajectory took a new turn when she accepted directorships of a number of public companies and associations including ANZ Banking Group (1983-94), Western Mining Corporation (1984-93), and the National Road and Motorists Association (1984-95). In some ways, 1988-89 was as decisive a year in her life as 1945 had been: in October of 1988, her husband, Harry, died of cancer, and she retired from her chair the following year, becoming an emeritus professor.

She had served as a Fellow of Senate at the University of Sydney in 1974-75, and, at the end of her career at the university, she returned to the Senate as Deputy Chancellor of the university from 1989 until 1991, when she was elected as Chancellor. She held that office until 2001, when she was forced to resign on pain of being removed from office by the Senate, which had lost confidence in her.

Her decade as Chancellor saw her remaining active in public life. In particular, she was appointed a non-parliamentary delegate to the Constitutional Convention convened at Old Parliament House, Canberra, in 1998, to consider whether Australia should become a republic. She had been actively involved with Australians for Constitutional Monarchy since its establishment in 1992, and, remaining a staunch opponent of the proposal to amend the Constitution to make Australia a republic, she was appointed to the No Case Committee responsible for running a publicly funded campaign against the proposal at the time of the 1999 referendum.

Her busy retirement activities were recognised with her appointment as a Companion of the Order of Australia in 1993 and the Centenary Medal awarded in 2003. Although she continued to live alone in her home in Vaucluse, she became increasingly frail, and, in 2011, she was admitted to Lulworth House with advanced dementia. She had been preparing her memoirs since 2002, although advancing dementia prevented her from finalising them. They were published under the title, *Broomstick: Personal Reflections of Leonie Kramer*, in 2012. She suffered a fall that year, after which her health continued to deteriorate until she died on 20 April 2016. She was given a state memorial service at the Sydney Conservatorium of Music (a college of the University of Sydney), at which the former Chancellor of the university, Dame Marie Bashir, delivered an address in the presence of the Governor of New South Wales, General David Hurley.

Speaking at the memorial service, her granddaughter, Tessa Dharmendra, provided a particularly affecting reflection on a woman who had not been emotionally demonstrative throughout her life. She spoke of the curious effect of dementia, and the way in which it seemed to release Kramer to engage emotionally in a way that had not previously been possible. On one occasion, when her granddaughter arrived to help her with some simple task, she rushed up to give her a hug. It was a simple gesture, but one that surprised a granddaughter who had come to accept her grandmother's emotional reticence. One can only be glad to think the cloud of dementia had something approaching a silver lining, and that there was some deepening of family bonds in these last years.

The emotional reticence was an important aspect of this lioness's armoury in public life, however, and it is well to remember that she prided herself on prioritising reason over emotion in public life. She fought the hard battles in public intellectual life to good effect. Thus, when the time came for her to retreat from the heat of battle, it is comforting to think that her personal life was able to develop in a way that happens when emotion triumphs over reason.

3
Learning

In the beginning of the 1970 academic year, "a statuesque middle-aged woman, with a flowing black gown, heavily embroidered on the sleeves, over a yellow and white dress" entered the University of Sydney's Wallace Lecture Theatre "and began to read in a beautifully modulated voice" from a book of Blake's poems:

"The Prophets Isaiah and Ezekiel dined with me, and I asked them how they dared so roundly to assert, that God spoke to them; and whether they did not think at the time, that they would be misunderstood, and so be the cause of imposition. Isaiah answer'd, I saw no God, nor heard any, in a finite organical perception; but my senses discover'd the infinite in every thing, and as I was then persuaded, and remain confirm'd; that the voice of honest indignation is the voice of God, I cared not for consequences but wrote."

Barry Spurr, who would forty years later become the first Professor of Poetry and Poetics in the university and the country, recalled the effect of this first lecture that he attended: "I sat there stunned. Perhaps others were stunned too, but I cared not a jot for them. I was, as the phrase goes, blown away. Then, Leonie Kramer began to unfold the mysteries of Blake's thought and how it was conveyed in both his prophetic books, such as this, and in the much simpler (although not simple) lyrics of the Songs, set for our study. This was what I had come to university for, and I was not disappointed. No concession was made to ignorance or subliteracy. I didn't feel 'safe'—

far from it, and I didn't want to feel 'safe'. I was shaken up. I had no sense of being 'supported', no intellectual truss was provided, and I didn't want or need it. I was being properly challenged and confronted; taken out of my too-comfortable comfort zone of school success; made (most importantly) patently aware of my almost total and profound ignorance, and introduced to a great poet. I was being initiated (through the dignified deportment, elegant articulation and brilliance of this lecturer, who understood that a lecture should be a polished performance, and who was an adult speaking respectfully to other adults, but without any faux-egalitarianism that would have been ludicrous under the circumstances) into what, once, was regarded as the university culture. That is, a grown-up world (not a nursery misconducted by nurturing nannies for victims of various kinds) that brought appropriate seriousness and high learning to complex intellectual concepts for the attention and stimulation of students capable of absorbing such material, but lucidly and comprehensibly too."

It was not only aspiring academics who benefited. In 1978, Santina Rizzo attended Kramer's lectures on *The Solid Mandala*. She was one of the many undertaking a BA, Dip.Ed. before embarking on a career as a high school teacher. She taught English for over three decades at Liverpool, Moorfield, and Wiley Park girls' high schools. As a working-class girl from Canterbury who had no idea who Kramer was, she remembers being struck by the sense that this was "someone pretty bloody powerful" whose clipped speech and highly structured lectures were still memorable forty years later, but also that "in the English Department, she was a standout educator—I know that now—I suppose I knew that at the time too." Rizzo recalls that the explicit discussion of language, character, and so on "lifted the words off the page" in a way that provided the blueprint for her own approach to high school English teaching: "I felt so supported in that novel study . . . she gave me the focus or scaffold that I needed."

Kramer had extensive experience in teaching before she came to Sydney. She had lectured and tutored students of English literature at the University of Melbourne, Hughes Hall, Oxford, and Canberra University College, as well as workingmen at Ruskin College in Oxford and science and engineering students at the University of New South Wales. To this was added her broadcasting experience for the ABC, and, indeed, experience as the mother of two daughters. All these perspectives she brought to bear when thinking about the nature of learning, education, and universities.

By the time she took the Chair of Australian Literature, she had clearly established for herself—if not others—that she was not a scholar content to work in an ivory tower. Indeed, she believed that "the notion of the ivory tower in which dedicated scholars lead contemplative lives, free of the taints and temptations of daily life, is a benign myth." When she saw practical problems that needed to be addressed, she was ready to step up to the mark. The domain in which she was most active concerned attitudes to 'learning'. In one sense, this was an intellectual debate about the correct way to approach the philosophy of education. In another way, however, it was a question of public policy: how should learning occur in state schools; how should learning be evaluated; and, ultimately, how should these answers influence questions to do with public funding for schools?

Progressive education and the 1960s

The Cold War shaped Kramer's experience of postgraduate life and her teaching career as much as the Second World War had been the dominant presence in the last years of her secondary schooling and the entirety of her undergraduate years. The values that underpinned these times were challenged by the permissiveness of the 1960s. Kramer was no wowser, but she did become concerned about the negative effects that she believed the developments of this decade were having on learning as 'progressive education' became fashionable.

In the philosophy of education, the ideas associated with progressive education date back at least as far as the late nineteenth century with the work of John Dewey, who was not only a leading light in the development of pragmatism in American philosophy, but also an influential educational theorist and practitioner. Dewey developed a new approach to education which emphasised the importance of the learner's experience as the centrepiece in what came to be known as progressive education. In the nineteenth century, the focus of education had been the acquisition of facts about the world. Dewey introduced the idea that the kind of experience that students have in the classroom significantly influences their understanding of what is being taught to them. He conceived of education as a journey of experiences. Dewey's purpose was to foster and cultivate a particular conception of community, however, over the course of the twentieth century, the focus shifted towards the primacy of the individual. With this shift, education was transformed so that the teacher served as a facilitator who enabled the students to assume control of their individual journeys within the classroom. It is beyond the scope of our present study to consider the nature of progressive education in any detail; to understand why it was thought to be important, and whether it had any beneficial effects. For present purposes, we must content ourselves with identifying the problems in education that Kramer attributed to the influence of the progressivists; what she did to combat these; and, in doing so, how she influenced public discourse.

One development that Kramer believed was critical to the way attitudes to education changed was the way in which the training of teachers was organised. The approach had been that an aspiring teacher would take a university degree that concentrated on the subject matter that the student hoped to teach before proceeding to a teachers' training college. There, the student would learn the skills necessary to give instruction about that subject matter in the classroom, and other skills associated with managing a classroom and effective teaching. Gradually, these independent training colleges transformed into faculties of education within universities. The transition from training colleges to education faculties saw teaching become a mainstream discipline within the humanities at a time when, Kramer maintained, humanities disciplines in general were moving in an unfortunate direction. It was a time when, she believed, excessive and unhelpful theorising became prevalent across the humanities.

Within the academic study of philosophy, 'metaphilosophy' refers to the philosophy of philosophy—the activity in which philosophers reflect upon what they are doing when they philosophise. This tendency to reflect theoretically on the nature of the discipline in which a scholar is immersed became prevalent across the humanities in the twentieth century as it became apparent that Hegel, Marx, Weber, Freud, and Foucault all offered intellectually exciting prospects for second-order reflection. Ordinarily philosophers, historians, economists, political scientists, archaeologists, art historians, musicologists, and professors of law and literature engage in first-order reflection on what the nature of reality is like, what people did in the past, how the economy or the legal system operates, or what art, music, and literature is created by people in different places and at different times. When these scholars embark on second-order reflection, they start theorising about such first-order reflection.

It would be wrong to suggest that this intellectual turn is itself pernicious—there are important questions to be asked, the significance of some of which might have been lost on Kramer. What she detected, however, was that this was having a pernicious effect in education. This was partly a result of what she regarded as 'fashionable' theorising that was prevalent in the humanities, and partly attributable to another tendency that she disparaged: the importing of ideas from abroad long after they had been challenged or even discredited in their place of origin. It was in this way that she believed theories of progressive education were able to take root in Australia.

Kramer acknowledged that there was a legitimate case for reform of education, explaining: "The concept of essential knowledge, exemplified by the curriculum of the ancient universities, no longer represented the growth of knowledge, and it was futile to resist change, which need not mean abandoning historical discoveries." What she objected to was the kind of change proposed by the progressivists, and the basis upon which they proposed these changes to education. Without providing a thorough account of what the educational progressivists were proposing in the 1960s within the parameters of this short study, it is still possible to grasp the key points that Kramer identified as problematic in their programme.

First, she believed that the 'fashionable' theorists were consumed by the 1960s' insatiable demand for *choice*, which, in the context of education, came to mean *liberation from requirements* as to what needed to be taught and learnt. Secondly, this vision of education was premised on what she regarded as a 'utopian' conviction that perfection is possible in any shared human endeavour, such as operating schools. Thirdly, there was a shift from *subject-centred* learning to *child-centred* learning. Finally, great value was attached to a particular understanding of *creativity*, which resulted in a situation in which it was important that children were given choices even though, Kramer believed, they lacked the capacity to evaluate the options they were being given.

Underlying this analysis are two central themes that Kramer found problematic. First, free thinking is treated as an end that is desirable in itself. Secondly, acquisition of knowledge is regarded as 'outmoded'. The combined effect of these two commitments is to debase an activity that Kramer calls 'criticism'. If the consequence of progressive education is a debasement of criticism, it is hardly surprising that this would be a matter of particular concern to Kramer, who had by this time made a name for herself as a literary critic. Criticism, for Kramer, is a matter of 'judging well' and this involves an exercise of knowledge. If 'free thinking' is a matter of expressing opinions without first exercising knowledge, it does not possess value for Kramer, because the opinions are only as good as the knowledge on which they are based. If the acquisition of knowledge is deemed to be outmoded and no longer to be taught, then it will not be possible for the student to have the necessary knowledge for judging well, and so the opinions that emanate out of the exercise of free thinking will lack value. In short, such free thinking does not amount to Kramer's sense of criticism, but rather serves only to diminish a student's capacity for criticism.

The approach of the 1960s progressivists also suffered, to her mind, from a more fundamental problem, namely the tendency towards abstraction. By inclination, Kramer does not seem to have been drawn towards abstraction. She was naturally disposed to understandings of the world that are derived from experience, rather than those that precede experience. Opinions lacking justification, she believed, were generally not helpful to clear thinking, particularly when applied to matters of social concern.

The philosophy of education is a theoretical pursuit, but it cannot long remain theoretical. Increasingly, Kramer sensed, education faculties within universities were assuming the role of teacher training previously undertaken in the training colleges. It followed that educational theory took on a practical dimension, as the professors of education encouraged the trainee teachers to adopt progressivist approaches when they went into the classroom. In this way, a theoretical issue about how to understand education became a practical issue about how to educate children when a teacher is standing in the classroom with them. In Australia, the state had assumed a central role in provision of education, assessment of educational achievement, and funding of schools operated independently of the state. Thus, the dispute about educational theory morphed into a public policy question as the state was required to make policy decisions about whether to support or oppose the progressivists' approach. Discussion about these points of public policy became political and this political dimension interested Kramer intensely.

Australian Council for Educational Standards

In 1966, the Victorian Department of Education formed the Curriculum Advisory Board for the purpose of making recommendations as to how the school curriculum might be revised in light of developments in educational theory and practice that had gained momentum internationally. This board was, in effect, the advocate for progressive education in Victoria. Although there were competing approaches to reform, the dominant one was the liberal humanism espoused by the Victorian Director of Secondary Education, R. A. Reed. Reed's liberal humanists believed that education should be directed towards the cultivation of the individual ('liberal') as a human capable of co-operation, self-reliance, problem-solving, and creativity ('humanist'). In terms of education, they believed that the desire to learn is innate, and that learners should have a meaningful and coherent experience of schooling. After Gough Whitlam won the federal election in 1972, the Labor government established the Australian Schools Commission to investigate the needs of government and non-government schools in order to ensure their longevity. The liberal humanist approach was embraced by the Australian Schools Commission's 1973 report, *Schools in Australia*. That same year, opponents of this approach formed the Australian Council for Educational Standards, under the leadership of James McAuley—a noted poet and friend of Kramer—in response to these developments, and with the specific purpose of resisting them.

Kramer accepted the presidency of the council and with it became the figurehead for what became characterized as the 'conservative' position in this public debate. It was a characterization that she knew had a strongly pejorative tinge to it, but she was prepared to wear this. Although the council and its members were presented as reactionaries who opposed change, Kramer was adamant that the conservatives were the true reformers, and that the progressives were really revolutionaries rather than reformers.

The Australian Council for Educational Standards shared much in common with the liberal humanist philosophy that it opposed, however, the points of difference were significant when it came to decisions about how children should be taught. Whereas the liberal humanists believed that children have an innate human drive to learn, and so can be left to their own devices in managing their own education, the council's membership tended to maintain that children, like all of us, are to some degree lazy, and need external stress—such as examinations—in order to apply themselves to learning and to assess what they have learnt. They also opposed the idea that subjects taught at school are merely samples of broader disciplines. Rather, they maintained that the subjects taught at school consist of bodies of substantiated facts and theories which have to be acquired as organised bodies of ordered knowledge through discipline and diligent learning.

At a time when liberal humanist views about education were very much in vogue in the 1970s, the council was highly effective in demonstrating that there were significant numbers of people opposed to the proposed reforms. They were effective in organising and publicising resistance to the proposed reforms, and drew attention to their weaknesses. Sometimes, they claimed, what seemed like a problem in the traditional or outmoded curriculum, when viewed from a theoretical perspective, was patently not a problem when viewed in terms of the practical contribution that it made to the child's life outside the school system.

Where they were less effective was in providing rigorous arguments. An opinion would be asserted, for instance, that 'standards are falling', but empirical evidence could not be adduced to support the opinion. Their purpose, however, was not to quantify or evaluate data. They did not deny the importance of such activities, but that was not the council's purpose. Its purpose was to be a voice in public policy debates; a noisy voice that insisted on being heard. This suited Kramer perfectly. Certainly, she was capable of detailed study of such problems, but that was not her preferred contribution to public discourse. She liked arguing for her 'strong views', and her style was to be forceful—verging on polemical.

The council sought to promote public awareness of educational problems; to resist the implementation of progressive education; to advocate for the best educational opportunity for each individual; and, to encourage opportunities for older people. What Kramer wanted to do was to establish that the conservatives were the true reformers and the progressives were the revolutionaries, whose agenda was ultimately destructive. In the spirit of Edmund Burke, she supported gradual reform of education; change in conformity with tradition. She was satisfied that in the five years that the Council was active, she and her colleagues "enjoyed some small but important victories." With the benefit of hindsight, some conservatives today would say that they won the battle but lost the war, as their influence was ultimately limited.

In the early 1990s, Kramer's advocacy moved to the Institute of Public Affairs, where she was made a senior fellow and oversaw the work of its newly established Education Policy Unit. The Institute of Public Affairs was established in 1943 by a number of prominent Melbourne businessmen who sought a vehicle through which they could influence public policy. Their primary purpose was to prevent the development of a 'new society' along socialist lines in the post-war reconstruction era.

The Education Policy Unit, which was funded through a substantial contribution from Ron Manners, was responsible for public advice on anything to do with the sector, from law and finance through to curriculum and teaching method. The unit comprised Susan Moore in Sydney and Ken Baker in Melbourne, who were overseen by Kramer. It undertook a three-year project that resulted in a report, *Educating Australians*, in 1992. Through this work, Kramer was able to influence the Hawke Government's approach to education and the Greiner Government's establishment of a Board of Studies in New South Wales to develop school curricula and maintain educational standards.

Kramer was satisfied that her work with the Australian Council for Educational Standards and the Institute of Public Affairs was successful in kerbing the excessive influence of progressive educationalists on public policy. For her, victory in this respect cannot be decisive. She would not presume to have the last word because, she accepted, there is no last word: "Progressive education advocates accused their opponents of looking in the rearview mirror, but they themselves looked neither back at history for useful lessons, nor ahead to anticipate the consequences of their theories. Real reformers do both, and they also recognise that there are no final answers to educational weaknesses."

Australian Universities Commission

Between 1959 and 1974, a series of Commonwealth statutes provided for an Australian Universities Commission and then in 1977 a Universities Council. The purpose of the commission and the council was to provide information and advice to the relevant federal minister on matters relating to Commonwealth financial assistance to universities, including the necessity for financial assistance to a specific institution, conditions upon which grants should be made, and the amount and allocation of financial assistance. Kramer was initially appointed a member of the Australian Universities Commission by the Whitlam Government, and continued to serve on it and its successor, the Universities Council, until 1986. Given the influence she had on the funding of universities, it is well to consider what it was that she thought universities should be funded to do.

There was a pragmatic dimension to Kramer's approach to universities. She rejected Cardinal Newman's approach in *The Idea of a University* (that a university is primarily a teaching, rather than a research institution, and one dedicated to the pursuit of knowledge for its own sake, through generalist rather than specialist education, so as to develop students' character), not simply because it was outdated, but because she thought there is no such thing as an ideal university. Universities exist in the real world, and they exist to address the needs of that world. So they are never the instantiation of some ideal but are always compromises that address competing real-world needs: she concluded that real-world institutions "must try to find a balance between the changing needs of students and the value of traditional knowledge."

Her conviction that progressive education has resulted in deficiencies in school education also had consequences for her pragmatic approach to universities. There is no point in assuming that students arrive at a university with an acquaintance with the canon when they have not been taught it. There is no point assuming they have levels of literacy or numeracy that they do not have. The university must adapt and respond to the needs of such students because this is the reality of students' experience at school.

She maintained that there are conceptual distinctions between education and training. These used to be the province of different kinds of institutions: universities on the one hand and training colleges and institutes of technology on the other. This distinction broke down when John Dawkins, Bob Hawke's Minister for Education and Training, introduced a unified national system that saw training colleges and institutes of technology either amalgamate as universities, or become absorbed into existing universities. The result is that, as a matter of fact, universities are now all involved in education and training to one degree or another. Thus, there is now little utility in pointing to conceptual differences that underpin different activities that would once have occurred within different institutions.

There was also a purist dimension to her thinking about universities. She believed that there is an activity that is unique to the university, and that is research. Schools, she believed, should not encourage pupils to undertake independent research. Their role is to prepare pupils to become students at university, where they will learn to undertake research, an activity that depends upon a firm understanding of existing knowledge. It is the role of the school to impart that knowledge in their pupils. This requires the pupil to be taught by another person—the teacher. It is only once one has been taught in this way, Kramer believed, that one is able to exercise independent judgement. It is at university that the pupil, who has graduated to become a self-directed student, can start to exercise independent judgement in a meaningful way.

The conviction that research is a distinctive activity of universities also influenced her conviction that universities that specialise in research—in Australia, the Group of Eight—ought to receive additional funding to enable them to carry out this research. To her way of thinking, universities that are the successor institutions to the old training colleges and institutes of technology really are second-tier universities and should be funded accordingly. To her mind, the Dawkins reforms may have created a single system of tertiary institutions, but they did not change the fact that the first-tier universities are the seat of research—the unique activity of universities—which requires appropriate funding, a view that persists in the Group of Eight research-intensive universities.

Her purist approach to the difference between schools and universities, and between research universities and other universities applies equally across the academic disciplines. There is another sense in which her purist approach applies to the humanities. She believed in a 'canonical tradition', or the idea that some books are better and more significant than others, and that this tradition needs to be the focus of teaching and learning in the humanities. This is at the core of what she regarded as 'cultural heritage'. Cultural heritage, she maintained, is not inert facts but knowledge about our heritage. "To know something is to possess what is known," she wrote in an essay entitled, 'A Heritage for Our Children', "so that it becomes part of one's way of thinking, embedded in the memory, always able to be activated for pleasure or to facilitate understanding and judgment." There is a reason why some writers and thinkers are designated as *great*, she maintains, and that is because they "have created our thoughts about the world as we know it." It is important, for Kramer, that they are *our* thoughts: the canon is valuable both to a person as an individual and to a community as a whole because it not only provides the individual with the capacity for critical judgment, but it also provides a sense of communal understanding. There is no doubt for her that the great books of the West are the ones that contribute "to our understanding of life and human experience" because "we are the inheritors of Greek, Roman and European thought and art." It might be objected that her approach leaves no room for Aboriginal and other non-Western literature in the canonical tradition. And yet her attachment to the English language does render her sensitive to the breadth of experience captured in English-language writing: "There could not be a better example of 'the living stream of culture' which now flows from the oldest Old English text to the latest West Indian novel or Aboriginal poem. Within the range of texts some are more important, some more accessible, and some of more educational value than others, and so professional decisions have to be made . . ."

She enjoyed relating a conversation with one of the first group of students from China after the Cultural Revolution. One of their number was perplexed by the way in which they were being taught at Sydney: they were being asked to express their opinions rather than to repeat what the teacher had said in lectures—as was the custom in Chinese institutions. She explained that "our universities were both conservative and radical: conservative in that they preserve and teach knowledge of the past, and radical in that they encourage an informed critique of the past." The student apparently responded to her, "The radical perspective would be very dangerous without the conservative one."

4
Literature

JOHN DOCKER, 35, who lived in Sydney and was the author of *Australian Cultural Elites*, wrote an article for *Overland* in 1981, entitled, 'Leonie Kramer in the Prison House of Criticism'. Towards the end of his somewhat catty commentary, he writes, "We might finally wonder how much Professor Kramer enjoys Australian literature, or literature as such . . . What *does* Professor Kramer find interesting about Australian literature?"

Although posed by a detractor, it is a fair question. Reflecting on her scholarly career, a long-time colleague in the English Department at the University of Sydney said, "I don't think Leonie really believed in Australian literature." Did Kramer believe that Australian literature existed, and, if so, did she believe it had any particular value?

Kramer's scholarly work centred on literary history and literary criticism. Literature, in its broader sense, is a body of written work, but, in its narrower sense, is a body of written work regarded as possessing artistic value. Literary history is the development over time of such work, and of the literary techniques employed in it. Literary criticism involves the comparison, analysis, interpretation, and evaluation. Although Kramer lectured on many aspects of literary history, her published work as an historian and critic concentrated on Australian literature. What is this Australian literature that interested her? In particular, are we to understand it as the development of a pre-existing literary tradition transplanted in Australia, or as a literature that provides a tool for giving expression to Australianness?

The English literary tradition

Kramer's interest in Australian literature lay particularly in understanding the way in which the main literary forms that emerged within the English literary tradition developed when they were transplanted in Australia. As for literary criticism, she once remarked that "It is no good praising a book for its plot or story or its lively characters unless you draw attention to the contribution it makes to the development of ideas *per se*, and to their literary expression."

Her own sensibilities align comfortably with a certain mode of criticism that is not overly emotional or overly intellectual. She acknowledged that she was not an 'emotional' person, as did her family when they spoke at her state memorial service. Equally, she was not given to 'intellectualising', as is seen in her hostility to overly theoretical approaches to understanding the human experience, and in particular in her advocacy about theoretical approaches to educational policy. Thus, although her approach to literature and criticism is deeply embedded within the English literary tradition, it is not so much in the tradition of the romantics or metaphysical poets, who are, perhaps, too emotional or too intellectual for her taste. Rather, her approach to criticism is very much informed by English authors and critics such as Dryden and Arnold.

John Dryden (1631-1700) was an English poet, dramatist,

and critic, whose essay, *Of Dramatick Poesie*, is often regarded as the first substantial piece of modern criticism. His style was at once lucid and conversational, and, indeed, established what we now regard as modern English prose. His appeal for Kramer lies in matter-of-fact prose that is neither overly intellectual, nor too emotional. This combination of lucid and robust language that is also conversational in tone is also a hallmark of Kramer's public speaking—notably her defence of the Australian Broadcasting Commission in her debate with the Minister for Communications in 1983.

Matthew Arnold (1822-1888) was an English poet, critic, and inspector of schools, whose essay, 'The Function of Criticism at the Present Time', sets out his conception of criticism and its role in society. By criticism, Arnold has in mind *evaluation* in the broadest sense, and this, he maintains, involves "a disinterested endeavour to learn and propagate the best that is known and thought in the world, and thus to establish a current of fresh and true ideas." He extends the activity of criticism beyond literature in its narrow sense: it involves the disinterested evaluation of ideas in all branches of learning. Kramer's adoption of this approach to criticism was unqualified. Its influence extends beyond her scholarship, however, to her engagement with educational policy reform, as witnessed in the title of an article she wrote for the *Sydney Morning Herald* on the subject in 1973: 'The Limits of Criticism'.

It is from the tradition of Dryden and Arnold that Kramer derived her life-long conviction that the value of literature lies in such virtues as lucidity, consistency, and rigorously holding to a line of argument; respect for formal aesthetics; demand for standards and the pursuit of excellence;

priority accorded to educated taste; and discernment, rationality, and clarity. This has consequences both for her understanding of the history of Australian literature and for her approach to criticism of Australian literature.

Henry Handel Richardson

Kramer's first significant contribution to the study of Australian literature was *Henry Handel Richardson and some of her sources*. This short monograph, which she completed en route to Oxford, is really an extended journal article with a set of appendices. Henry Handel Richardson was the pen name of Ethel Florence Lindesay Richardson (1870-1946), a novelist born in Melbourne to parents of Irish ancestry, but who spent the last six decades of her life abroad, mostly in England, where she never felt at home; but also in Germany, where she felt happiest. The *Australian Dictionary of Biography* describes her place in Australian literature as "important and secure." Her novel, *The Fortunes of Richard Mahony*, was conceived as a fictionalised study of her father and his descent into insanity, but the novelist's husband observed that it was more a study of her own life than her father's. Kramer had access to unpublished Richardson materials relating to the novel, which had been deposited with the National Library in Canberra. In particular, there were two notebooks, in which Richardson recorded her historical research, an index she made of the material contained in the two notebooks, and a diary that she kept during a visit to Australia in 1912 to record the places and landscapes where her father had lived and to check her memories of places she recalled from childhood. Kramer carefully analysed the way the notebooks and diary reveal Richardson's use of fact—both historical and perceptual—

in her novel, *The Fortunes of Richard Mahoney*.

Kramer's study demonstrates her impressive capacity for detailed analysis of primary sources. She is able to show how Richardson gathered facts and then incorporated them into a novel, and, indeed, the significance of her use of the facts for the novel's literary value. In the end, she concludes that Richardson's approach to facts at critical moments in the novel diminishes it. She explains that "It is unfortunately true that at moments when the novel can least afford it, Richardson produces the commonplace . . . I do not mean to suggest that Richardson ought not to be accurate in her descriptions, but that their accuracy should not be their chief, least of all their only, recommendation. [D. H.] Lawrence can be accurate and preserve the magic of his scenes; Richardson needs to do the same if the tone of the novel is to be sustained. If we are to realize the effect of the Australian landscape on Mahony's restless and irritable temperament, Richardson must do more than tell us where to look for the You-Yangs and Creswick Creek. It may be that she can do no more than this, or that she thinks no more than this is necessary; in either case she is at fault, and the novel as a whole suffers from what one can only call a failure of imagination."

Kramer's close analysis of Richardson's passages of description allows her to expose both the novelist's methods and weaknesses: "Richardson's failures are not so much failures of intellect as failures of vision. When her eye should be on the distant horizon it is busy in the foreground counting gum trees, not so that they will add depth and perspective to the completed picture, but so that we shall know just how many gum trees there are . . . Richardson grasps intellectually ideas which show a particular understanding of human conflicts, but fails, as Mahony himself fails, when it comes to their realization. To say how she could have succeeded is neither necessary nor possible. One can only point to a man like Dostoevsky who succeeded eminently and say, 'That is how it is done.'" For all that, she is circumspect about the failings: "to have fallen short of the highest achievement is not to have wholly failed; and nothing is more harmful to Richardson's real merits than false and inflated comparisons with writers whose work is on a different level."

Despite its shortcomings, Kramer maintains that *The Fortunes* does have literary merit. In drawing this conclusion, she does not believe that this is because it exemplifies literary nationalism or social realism—two approaches to literary criticism that she strenuously rejects. Literary nationalism is exemplified by Vance Palmer in *The Legend of the Nineties*. The literary nationalists attach literary value to literature that promotes nationalist sentiments. Henry Lawson was seen by some as doing this in the 1890s, when certain virtues of life in the bush, such as mateship, were identified as quintessentially Australian virtues worthy of celebration as such. In her introduction to the *Oxford History of Australian Literature*, Kramer regards a preoccupation with national identity as "imitative": "It is a common notion, pursued at certain stages of their history, by many countries. Even in a country with a long cultural tradition, it resists definition. In Australia, whose literary history is less than two hundred years old, any attempt to define national characteristics is bound to be more an expression of hopes and possibilities than an historical statement." She suggests that Palmer does not describe the Australian national character, so much as he selects those aspects that fit with his view of the 'real' Australia.

On the one hand, she thinks a country like Australia is too complicated to have its character defined: "At the centre of [Palmer's] thinking were ideas of character and ways of life which, at the time he was writing, were only part—and a diminishing one—of a much more complex whole." On the other hand, she rejects the idea that Australian literature should be concerned with what is authentically Australian because "Literary values are made to depend upon notions as to the proper subjects and attitudes for an Australian writer to take."

Australian literary criticism

Social realism attaches literary value to literature's capacity to articulate the actual social or political condition of people. Even in the 1890s, few Australians lived in the bush, and the world that Lawson evoked was not the actual world in which Australians lived. The social realists value literature as a vehicle for commentary about the ills of the political state and civil society in which people actually live. Kramer eschewed this approach to literature, which she saw taking hold in fiction and drama—but not poetry—with what she regarded as unfortunate consequences: "the sacrifice of artistry to mundane detail, of the exploration of character to assertions about stereotypes, of style to what Patrick White called 'dun-coloured' journalism or to lively but brittle colloquialisms."

Kramer's dispute with the literary nationalists and the social realists was a dispute about what contributed to literary value. Another dispute, however, centred on Australian critics' capacity to make mature judgements about their native literature. 'The Cultural Cringe' was the name of a celebrated article by A. A. Phillips published in *Meanjin* in 1950. In it, Phillips puts forward the thesis that Australian critics lack the cultural maturity to make objective judgements about their compatriots' works of art because they are always prone to ask the question, "Yes, but what would a cultivated Englishman think of this?" He thinks this demonstrates the lack of cultural maturity amongst Australian critics but it goes beyond mere insecurity: Australian authors should be writing for Australian audiences, he maintains, and so the response of a cultivated foreign audience is not relevant to the evaluation of Australian literature. The critic, he believes, must be confident to judge how a work speaks to an Australian audience.

Kramer's rejection of the cultural cringe is twofold. First, drawing on L. J. Hume's *Another Look at the Cultural Cringe*, she thinks the argument fails: Phillips "makes assumptions which are not supported by evidence, and seems at times to express personal *animus* instead of arguing a case." Secondly, she rejects it as a matter of fact. Where some see the cultural cringe in play in the work of the likes of Mrs Campbell Praed and Henry Handel Richardson, Kramer sees no trace of it. For Kramer, Phillips represents a colonial mindset that is hostile to Australia's English—but not Scottish or Irish—settlers and which recognises "none of the benefits of Australia's cultural heritage" derived from England.

Australian literary history

The Oxford History of Australian Literature stands as a monument to Kramer's scholarship, although it is not entirely clear what kind of monument it is. She would say it was a reassertion of an approach to literature that had become unfashionable. Others would say that she and her co-authors occupied a position of power within the academy, and this was an expression of their authority. The volume consists of an introductory essay by Kramer as the general editor and three extended essays by contributors chosen by her—Adrian Mitchell, Terry Sturm, and Vivian Smith—all members of the English Department at the University of Sydney, together with a bibliography compiled by Joy Hooton. The extended essays trace the development of the three main literary forms in Australia since 1788: fiction, drama, and poetry.

The work was not well received by reviewers and there were several lines of objection. Although it describes Les Murray as "among the best poets the country has produced," he did not repay the compliment. Writing in *Island Magazine*, he calls out the book's "aesthetic and anti-nationalist" bias which is "scornful of literary Australianism and the vernacular dimension," suggesting that "If this were a 1920s book about American music, it would still be resisting jazz." Some objections were more petty—grievances by those who felt they were unjustly left out. Then there were the more serious criticisms that Kramer's introduction anticipated regarding the decision to exclude literary forms other than the three main ones. Finally, there were objections that the volume ignores the impact of the *isms* on criticism—which appears to have been a deliberate editorial decision.

That the breadth of literature taken in was too narrow was a criticism that Kramer had anticipated. H. M. Green's monumental two-volume *History of Australian Literature:*

Pure and Applied had demonstrated the range of writing in Australia that could be assessed as part of a history of Australian literature by 1961: the literature of science, psychology, economics, philosophy, journalism, history, biography, travel, and reminiscence. Despite this, Kramer felt justified in adopting a narrower focus. Her decision was partly pragmatic—she needed to keep the work to a single volume. There was more to it than that, however: underlying the pragmatic decision was a deeper belief that the trajectory of the literary tradition is seen to best advantage by studying the principal literary forms of that tradition across time and place. Others might object that this was a form of cultural snobbery, but Kramer was upfront about the fact that she regarded it as a legitimate historical perspective.

The criticism that the *Oxford History* fails to address the insights of feminism, postcolonialism, Aboriginal studies, and a range of other theoretical perspectives is not addressed directly by Kramer. She was undoubtedly aware of the work that was being done in these subfields and made a deliberate decision to ignore it. In a sense this is unsurprising. She had an innate suspicion of overly abstract or theoretical approaches to the humanities. Combined with this suspicion was a deep conviction that non-literary considerations were not relevant to assessments of literary merit, and issues such as the social condition of women or the dispossession and discrimination endured by indigenous peoples were, to her mind, non-literary considerations.

What is it then that Kramer thinks is the business of literature? In short, the human condition. The highest purpose of literature, for Kramer, is to explore the inner recesses of the soul, the psyche, character. Over the centuries, the English literary tradition has refined the novel, the poem, and the drama as vehicles for exploring what it is to be human. The poets and novelists she admired most in Australia were those who demonstrated an ability to develop the tradition in some way by developing a personal style that allowed them to say something about what it meant to be human—in Australia. Unless Australians are qualitatively different from other human beings, this will not be a claim about what it means to be Australian. It will be a claim about what it means to be human. In doing so, Australian writers might well draw on distinctly Australian experiences in order to reveal something about the human experience.

Literary greatness, for Kramer, lies not just in the subject matter, but in the treatment of the subject matter. To be sure, she thought that the investigation of the human psyche was the proper subject of great literature. Literary greatness is more than that, however. It is revealed in the development of a writer's personal style. A personal style arises when there is a formal development of the tradition. So the critic's role is then to have a command of the literary tradition, and to explain how a particular work evinces a personal style that is a unique development of the tradition.

She believed that Australian poets really started to achieve this in the 1940s, and those whose work she most admired also happened to be personal friends, most notably the Catholic poet, James McAuley (1917-1976) and the satirical poet, A. D. Hope (1907-2000). Novelists, she believed, got going a bit earlier, in the 1930s, with the novels of Christina

Stead (1902-1983) and Patrick White (1912-1990), although she also regarded Henry Handel Richardson as a novelist in this tradition.

Patrick White

When it comes to Patrick White, it is hard to tell the fact from the legend. Their paths rarely crossed, and yet the literary establishment rejoiced in tittle-tattle about the conflict between these two doyens. For all the hostility, she did write about his literary achievements as well as explaining what she found problematic in his work. It was a curious situation in which she was, perhaps, as startled to find much of value in him as he was horrified to think that she could find value in his work.

From the outset, Kramer was tainted by association in White's estimations. She was a close personal friend of A. D. Hope, about whom she had written approvingly and whose literary sensibilities she shared. In 1956, Hope published a review of White's *The Tree of Man* in the *Sydney Morning Herald*, which, however otherwise balanced it might have been, contained the following sentence: "When so few Australian novelists can write prose at all, it is a great pity to see Mr White, who shows on every page some touch of the born writer, deliberately choose as his medium this pretentious and illiterate verbal sludge." David Marr writes in his biography, "No shaft of criticism ever wounded White so deeply. He raged against Hope as a peacock, a dingo in a pack whose spite knew no bounds, and 'an embittered schoolmaster and a poet of a *certain* distinction'." Marr suggests that, as a result of this episode, "White's suspicion of academics—including Hope's friend

Leonie Kramer—now turned into set antagonism. He was never quite as hostile as he wished to appear."

Kramer's actions undoubtedly contributed as much as her associations. In 1964, she was commissioned by Angus & Robinson to edit their biennial collection of short stories, *Coast to Coast*. In assembling the collection, she included stories by the leading authors of the day with the exception of White, who did not appear in the collection. This omission was drawn to Kramer's attention by her publisher, Douglas Stewart. She maintains that she reviewed the decision and concluded that the omission was in order and the collection not in need of revision. This appears to have inflamed White. It was seen by many discerning readers as a singular omission. Some were content to believe that a scholar of her standing must have had a legitimate reason; others, that this was some personal vendetta. In 1979, she told *The Bulletin*, "Now I think it may have been an incorrect decision."

In the end, she could do no right in his eyes. When she wrote congratulating him on receiving the Nobel Prize, White could only snipe to others about how short the letter of congratulation was. In his autobiography, *Flaws in the Glass*, White wrote of "those who are unequivocally male or female—and Professor Leonie Kramer." We might wonder both what he means and why he formed this conclusion. In terms of what the passage means, it is often parsed in isolation, but it is well to consider it in the context of the preceding passage: "I sometimes wonder how I would have turned out had I been born a so-called normal heterosexual male ... As a woman, I might have been an earth-mother ... Or I might have chosen a whore's life . . . Or else a nun, of milky complexion and sliced-white bread smile, dedicated to her quasi-spiritual marriage with the most demanding spouse of all. Instead, ambivalence has given me insights into human nature, denied, I believe, to those who are unequivocally male or female..." White presents his own situation as the predicament of a homosexual man in a heterosexual man's world. Kramer was a heterosexual woman in that heterosexual man's world. There is schoolboy nastiness in the suggestion that this woman does not display unambiguously feminine qualities, but there is also a sense in which it exposes a greater degree of similarity between their respective predicaments than either might care to admit. What becomes clear, however, is that where White gained insight from the ambivalence that was his predicament, Kramer did not. If anything, she was determined not to acknowledge that the predicament had afforded her any special insight.

In 1963, *Quadrant* published its first article about Patrick White. In it, H. P. Heseltine attempted to explain why White's prose is not 'illiterate verbal sludge'. Heseltine distinguishes between the approach taken in White's earlier novels and the later novels, which evidence his mature style. He explains that "by the time he wrote *The Aunt's Story* White had pretty thoroughly developed those elements of his style which give it its characteristic emotional attitudes, tone, and texture. From an uncommonly fecund sensibility he had extrapolated certain interlocking images, metaphors, and symbols, which provided him with a vocabulary capable of great subtlety in dealing with personal relationships and inner states of mind... If we combined the elements of this preparation with the notion of a syntax calculated to render, before all else, streams of individual consciousness, we might arrive at a fairly accurate account of White's style up to this point in his career. White's early novels, in other words, are in the main uncommitted novels of sensibility."

In *The Tree of Man*, Heseltine finds the beginnings of White's mature style. In *The Aunt's Story*, White had already shown an interest in the idea that wisdom and knowledge are found in insanity; something unavailable to those content with 'common sense'. Madness, White maintains, allows access to 'intuition' or 'illumination'. Heseltine opines that "For such a view to make any kind of sense, it requires that man have a soul and that there be a God, or at least some kind of divine force, to make the intuition and illumination possible. I do not know what, as a man, Patrick White now believes, or what he believed before he wrote *The Tree of Man*; but that is his first novel to accept, as an axiom, the duality of man's nature and the existence of a divine spirit. Such a belief, it seems to me, is the only possible next step after *The Aunt's Story*; while *The Aunt's Story* was the only possible result of White's initial explication of his sensibility into image, metaphor, and situation."

On Heseltine's understanding of White's transcendental project, far from being verbal sludge, "his style is the very linchpin of what he has to say." It is precisely through his use of language that he is able to give expression to his ideas. The idiosyncrasies of White's syntax, according to Heseltine, "have more than anything else caused uneasiness, even among White's admirers. Certainly, some of his sentences do exhibit an odd structure, at times even violate the canons of accepted grammar. But the violations are not haphazard; there is a pattern to the oddity of structure, and the pattern is directly germane to White's meaning. Thus, White's punctuation has always been eccentric." In White's mature style, "The punctuation now functions to enforce attention on the individual moment, to insist on its metaphysical significance; in short, to suggest that while experience may be continuous, some parts of it are more important than others."

Ten years later, *Quadrant* published 'Patrick White's Götterdämmerung', an article by Kramer which challenged such interpretations of White's metaphysical project. Although critics like Heseltine have understood White to be defining the nature of visionary experience and the relationship between visionaries and their society in his mature novels, Kramer argues that "far from endorsing transcendentalism, White is offering a critique of it." She believes that the preoccupation in the mature novels "has been to ask how man comes to discover that he himself has invented God; how he reacts to his discovery; and what its consequences are." Through a close study of *Riders in the Chariot*, Kramer concludes that the thesis of the novel is that "man is the measure of all things. His search for the truth about his own condition will not be assisted by notions about a reality beyond the world of appearances. The world of appearances *is* that reality. Therefore, to say that 'God is in this table' is not to say that God is immanent (and possibly transcendent as well). It is to say that there are not two levels of reality, but one."

In this way, Kramer rejects Heseltine's interpretation of the mature novels as expressions of transcendentalism for which White's difficult and idiosyncratic style is necessary in order to enable him to treat his themes. In contrast, she maintains that White's novels are a project in humanist materialism—not transcendentalism or immanent divinity. In a sense, however, she does agree with Heseltine about the significance of White's style for his project. She can see that he uses language in a distinctive way that is critical to his project. On her analysis, however, this is a weakness—rather than a strength—of his novels. Critics would not have seen *Riders in the Chariot* as an essay in transcendentalism, she explains, "had they not been encouraged by its action, imagery, and language to do so. White's intellectual commitment is to humanism and to scepticism of transcendent or mystical notions and sanctions, but the novel discloses an emotional attraction to mystery and the irrational. Anxious though White is to give substance and depth to purely humanistic values ... he also wants to represent them as more-than-ordinary." It is at this point that she believes his use of language, though seemingly effective, is in fact problematic: "This can be accomplished by applying the language of religion to the mundane affairs of his illuminates. But it is difficult to use the language of religious experience without seeming to suggest that it has content as well as form." Although she does not go so far as to pronounce his prose to be verbal sludge, she does conclude that "In this way his style subtly undermines his subject, and there are many instances of verbal effects masking a weakness in observation or psychological motivation." Thus, Kramer concludes that, for White, "One of the consequences of the death of God may be loss of faith in the Word."

The death of God worried Kramer. She told Craig McGregor that she struggled with White's position, explaining, "You have to hold on to the belief that God isn't dead, in order to provide that dimension which is non-material ..." But how was she to do this? Perhaps, Barry Spurr's recollection of

Kramer quoting Blake's Isaiah is the means of holding on: "I saw no God, nor heard any... but my senses discover'd the infinite in every thing..." William Blake (1757-1827) was one of the English poets for whom Kramer felt the greatest admiration. His poems offer visions of the transcendent derived from intuition rather than doctrine. Although he was deeply religious, he eschewed organised religion, so it is unsurprising that a 'leftover' like Kramer might find in his poetry the transcendent denied by White's later novels. That Blake should offer her the experiences of the transcendent that White does not raises new puzzles. In literature, it has been noted that Dryden served as her model, much as Burke did for her in politics. Yet neither of these eighteenth-century figures are noted for offering the experiences found in Blake. This suggests a disconnect, at the least, between her thinking about prose and politics on the one hand, and religion and poetry on the other. It suggests a dichotomy in her belief system that might warrant further investigation.

What is apparent is that Kramer can see in White an author who is relating to the literary tradition in the way that she expects a major writer to relate to it. He is using the literary form to explore the ultimate nature of the human condition, and he has done so through the development of a personal style that extends the tradition. It cannot be denied, however, that Kramer was critical of White's work, and the criticism comes to the fore when she evaluates the personal style that he cultivates. White seems to have been contemptuous of any criticism from within the academy. It needs to be borne in mind, however, that Kramer saw this as the role of the critic. It is also worth remembering that her criticism of White is in the same vein as that of

Richardson: in her earliest writing, she was quite frank about the way in which Richardson's use of fact could—at critical moments such as Mahony's moment of vision about the meaning of life—undermine her writing.

Home thoughts from abroad

In 1982, Kramer wrote 'Home thoughts from abroad' for *Quadrant* whilst she was at Harvard. She was forthright in her contempt for the state of literary criticism in Australia, and whether or not she had Docker's *Overland* article in mind, his article embodies the criticism she railed against: "[it is] the tone of much Australian criticism, whether from authors, academics or journalists, which is most offensive. It is smug, abrasive, and patronising, frequently treating the reader as though he is a backward pupil, needing to be lectured at and rebuked for inattentiveness to the pearls being cast before him." Such comments reveal why, however courteous colleagues found her to be, her manner was also divisive, and disdain developed—especially amongst those who did not know her personally.

There were two sources of conflict that Kramer provoked in her scholarly career. The first came from her understanding of what mattered about Australian literature, namely that it was the development of a venerable English tradition within Australia. This conception of Australian literature meant that she was at odds with the social realists and literary nationalist authors, and those critics who lamented what they saw as the cultural cringe. The other conflict, with Patrick White, stemmed less from disagreements about the nature and purpose of Australian literature than from her evaluation of his style, given their shared understanding of the literary endeavour in Australia.

Kramer demanded that we acknowledge the best that our tradition has achieved, and judge the contribution of contemporary writers according to the tradition's standards. She was at her best when defending the tradition and contemporaries who contributed to its development. In this, she was very much at home with Burke's conception of tradition as a source of guidance. Like some conservatives, however, she risked becoming unstuck by the ever-present risk of lurching into reactionary responses.

Like Burke, she might have been right to resist changes to the tradition based on abstract theorising such as postcolonialism and feminism. In doing so, however, she seems to have failed to acknowledge that the tradition itself became increasingly concerned with the experience of Aboriginal people and women in Australia, and that this might have been a legitimate development of the literary tradition, even if postcolonialism and feminism as ideological approaches had little to offer. At a time when many in the academy and society at large were enthusiastically shunning tradition of any sort, Kramer was an unashamed advocate for tradition as a source of standards in literature. Such a commitment has its blinkers, however, and the *Oxford History of Australian Literature* suggests Kramer was little concerned by the way in which these might limit her appreciation of the legitimate ways in which the tradition was developing in Australia. Yet such blinkers do not John Docker's prison house make.

5

Law, society and culture

THE TWILIGHT OF Dame Leonie Kramer began in 2001, when the Senate of the University of Sydney took steps to remove her from the Chancellorship. Her apotheosis had come in 1991, when she was installed as the fifteenth Chancellor of the university. For four decades, Kramer had taken an active interest in society, culture, and matters of state. She engaged with them as a public figure, but she also reflected on them. In terms of Australian society, which we might regard as the sum of our varied conditions and activities functioning interdependently, she broke ground as the first woman to serve in a number of prominent positions and offered unexpected commentary on feminism from that perspective. As for culture—the arts and other manifestations of society's intellectual achievement—her scholarship took her into aspects of Australian culture focussed on literature, and she played a wider part in public discussions as a judge for the Miles Franklin Literary Prize and as chairman of *Quadrant*'s board of directors. When it comes to the Australian state—the structure through which society is an organised political community under one system of government—she played an influential role in discussions about the state's role in censorship and public broadcasting, most notably as chairman of the ABC, and also in constitutional matters through her involvement in the debate about whether Australia should become a republic. With all this behind her, she could not comprehend that she should have been deprived of the Chancellorship in the way that she was and spent her remaining years ruminating on this as dementia engulfed her—she could not let go of it.

Chancellorship of the University of Sydney

The University of Sydney was established by an act of the legislature of New South Wales in 1850. It was the first university to be established on the Australian continent. The governing body of the university is its Senate, which comprises the Chancellor, Vice-Chancellor, presiding member of the Academic Board, seven external fellows, five fellows selected by the staff, and two selected by the students. The Senate elects the Chancellor, who presides over it, and is the ceremonial figurehead of the university. Until 2001, the Senate had the power to appoint the Chancellor and to remove the Chancellor on the grounds of incapacity—but not on the grounds that a competent Chancellor had lost the Senate's confidence. In that year, the university obtained the approval of the Governor of New South Wales for an amendment to its by-laws to give the Senate the power to remove the Chancellor if a motion of no confidence in the Chancellor were passed at two successive meetings of the Senate.

Kramer had presided over the Senate that appointed Professor Gavin Brown as Vice-Chancellor in 1996. She subsequently agreed to a re-negotiation of the Vice-Chancellor's remuneration in a way that was advantageous to him. It was alleged that, in doing so, she failed to observe the correct procedures, which would have involved referring the matter to the Senate's remuneration committee. This was the technicality on which her enemies could get her. They said they no longer had confidence in her, on account of the way she had managed this change in the Vice-Chancellor's remuneration, and, as such, she should resign. She refused to resign. So the Senate obtained the power to remove her.

The proposed by-law had been considered by the NSW parliamentary Regulation Review Committee, which approved it by a narrow majority, and so the Minister for Education, John Aquilina, advised the Governor to grant formal approval. This was justified on the basis that the government should not interfere with a university's autonomy, provided there was no legal impediment to the proposed by-law. To rush through such a significant change in order to remove a specific person is an extraordinary action for a public institution to take. The pretext for the motion of no confidence was the mismanagement of the renegotiation of the Vice-Chancellor's remuneration, but this alone could not have provided the motivation for changing the by-laws. So two questions arise: Why were the fellows of Senate determined to remove Kramer in the way that they did? and Why did she respond to their threat in the way that she did?

It is not hard to see why the fellows might have reached the conclusion that Kramer was no longer a good 'fit' for the university. She, no doubt, modelled herself on her immediate predecessors, Sir Hermann Black and Sir James Rowland. They were widely respected figures, but they were also essentially non-partisan figures.

Kramer maintained that she was not a party-political figure, despite having taken forthright stances in public debates of a political nature, but this became increasingly harder to justify. It is true that she was never a member of the Liberal Party, but she was identified with the politics of John Howard. She played a prominent part in the campaign to oppose making Australia into a republic, and, again, although this was not strictly a party-political debate, it was a quasi-political debate. She also attracted attention for stances such as her repudiation of the feminists' claims that a 'glass ceiling' impeded women's employment opportunities, including in universities.

Such involvement in public discourse had two consequences. Whether or not one agreed with her stances, it was increasingly difficult to claim that she was non-partisan. Secondly, the fact of the matter was that the tide of opinion within the academy and Sydney high society had changed. Both were less conservative than they had been a couple of decades earlier. Academics, particularly in the humanities and social sciences, had increasingly drifted towards progressive—if not postmodern—agendas. Those who exerted power and influence in Sydney society no longer identified with traditional institutions and values that would once have been associated with the establishment. Thus, it is not hard to see why she was no longer an appropriate figurehead for the university, given how out of keeping she was with the prevailing ethos and politics of the academy and the Senate.

Sydney's high society has always been deeply attached to the university and its Chancellorship has remained an important social position. To see this, one need only look at the kind of person who has occupied it. As the power centres in Sydney society have shifted, so too has the identity of the Chancellor: it moved from pastoralists to professionals, academics, and businessmen and women. This is significant because, by the turn of the twenty-first century, Kramer was far from the darling of fashionable society. Its values and politics had drifted away from hers.

That the fellows of Senate might have resolved to appoint a different kind of person when her term expired in 2003 was understandable enough. That they were not prepared to endure her for a further two years speaks to other motivations. John Howard recalls that the mood of the country in the 1990s was such that prominent people were ridiculed for being monarchists. He suggests that what he regards as the "unreasonable derision" directed at Tony Abbott was primarily a response to his public stance on the monarchy. Michael Lavarch revealed that Paul Keating resisted appointing Michael Kirby to the High Court because he was a monarchist (and he only agreed, according to Lavarch, when it was pointed out that appointment to the High Court would silence him and so deprive the monarchists of their greatest weapon). Lloyd Waddy, who founded Australians for Constitutional Monarchy with Kirby, suffered heavily for his stance. Thus, there is reason to conclude that Howard is right that an element of personal revenge cannot be discounted in understanding the attack on Kramer. It is consistent with the way that other prominent monarchists were treated at this time and suggestive of a form of intolerance in political and academic life that emerged in the following decades.

Kramer was inclined to see this whole episode through the lens of governance. She thought that others either did not understand how the university's governance structure worked, or that they were trying to usurp it (whereas some of those others found her to be contemptuous of the Senate). Certainly, she fought hard, recruiting support wherever she could find it, and she mounted a public counteroffensive using her connections in the media, law, and politics. She had lost the support of the governing body, however, and even the Vice-Chancellor was powerless to save her in the end.

Why did she fight on? There was, no doubt, an element of pride. There was also a conviction that she had the university's best interests at heart. Her sense of the university's best interests was increasingly at odds with that of the fellows of Senate, academics, and students. They largely disagreed with her stances on the republic, on education and learning, on Australian culture and nationhood, and women's experience of the workforce. In the end, she agreed to stand aside as Chancellor before the second motion of no confidence was passed, but there is no way around the fact that she was forced to vacate the office, and that she was unable to do so on her own terms. And there is no doubt that there had been a changing of the guard: she was no longer wanted because the culture that she represented was no longer valued within the university.

It is hard to avoid the conclusion that this was a humiliating end to a distinguished public life. Kramer had been the first woman appointed to a chair at the University of Sydney. She was prominent in public broadcasting, big business, and government advisory roles long before women's presence was being felt in these arenas. In part, this was because broadcasters, businessmen, and policymakers saw in Kramer a woman with whom they could do business;

a clear-eyed, sensible, no-nonsense sort of person whose values they shared. Of course, there were still people who respected her and shared her values, but they were becoming more marginal; more marginal, at least, within the academy and the social stratum that dominated the university's Senate.

Censorship

Information and ideas were central to Kramer's teaching and research activities, so it was natural that she should come to think about the state's role in the dissemination of information and ideas. There are two obvious ways in which the state can influence such dissemination. It can try to prevent the dissemination, most obviously through censorship. It can also try to promote the dissemination, such as through public broadcasting.

Censorship was a topic that had entered her scholarship at Oxford, when she studied formal satire in England between 1590 and 1650. Much of the literature that interested her during this period was created in response to state censorship, and the need to circumvent it by writing satirically about topics that could not otherwise be discussed. This gave her a background that meant she felt confident to accept an invitation to be appointed to the National Literature Board of Review in 1971.

The board was created in 1968 to advise customs officers whether any written material that had been imported and seized, and which they would otherwise be obliged to destroy, might contain literary merit. She claimed not to have any particular views on censorship when she accepted the position. What did strike her was the enduring relevance of Milton's *Areopagitica* (1644). Milton continued to be cited by politicians, such as Don Chipp, when he wanted to explain the difference between 'freedom' and 'licence' in 1970, and the enduring need for some limited form of censorship.

As it happened, her time on the board was cut short when it was abolished by Gough Whitlam's Attorney-General, Lionel Murphy, in 1972. Kramer found his manner objectionable, as he dined with the board but did not indicate that he was about to abolish it, leaving them to read about it in the next day's newspapers. It was not the abolition of the board that she lamented, but the way it was abolished: she maintained that he had acted decisively but without providing any justification. This left Kramer feeling that three centuries after Milton, what had changed was not the fact that a free press was still important, but that arguments were no longer required to justify why it was important. This, she regretted.

ABC

Public broadcasting had entered Kramer's career soon after she returned to Australia. As early as 1956, she was broadcasting on ABC radio for The Critics and then for Any Questions. The knowledge that she would be able to draw on this experience gave her confidence when she was appointed a commissioner of the ABC in 1977, and subsequently its chairman in 1982. It seems that Malcolm Fraser's Minister for Communications, Ian Sinclair, had initially approached two other people who declined the offer to become chairman, and so the outgoing chairman, John Norgard, and the general manager, Sir Talbot Duckmanton, encouraged the minister to consider Kramer.

By this time, Kramer was known for her conservative views, and those who thought that the Fraser administration had appointed her to steady the ship by pushing the ABC further to the right were to be disappointed. For most of her short tenure as chairman, she found herself dealing with a Labor Government in Canberra, and defending what might be regarded as 'leftist' critique of the Labor Government. Two key themes stand out in her approach to public broadcasting. The critical one is the relationship between the government and the national broadcaster, in which the latter must be ever vigilant to assert its independence from the former, notwithstanding that this is the source of its funding. Secondly, she was committed to 'excellence' or 'standards' in broadcasting. Such excellence, she believed, was critical to maintaining the correct relationship between the government and the public broadcaster: the higher the standard of the broadcaster's output, the more commanding it could be in asserting its independence of the government.

In June 1981, *The ABC in Review: National broadcasting in the 1980s—Report by the Committee of Review of the Australian Broadcasting Commission* was published. It was known as the Dix Report after the committee's chairman, Alex Dix. It was intended to inquire into all aspects of the public broadcaster's operations in order to review its future. Kramer had been part of the committee of commissioners that prepared a submission for the review. The submission proposed, amongst other things, that the ABC should be permitted to have advertising and sponsorship of programmes. This was one of a number of wide-ranging changes that were recommended in the report, including that the ABC should be run as a commercial enterprise, and that it should narrow down the scope of its activities, for instance by giving up management of the orchestras it had founded.

The Fraser Government's response to the Dix Report, and the Commission's response to the government's response was central to perceptions of Kramer's two-year tenure. The staff were deeply hostile to the idea that the ABC could ever have advertising or sponsorship, and the new chairman's openness to this was viewed with deep suspicion. Her response to the Dix Report was nuanced, however. Although she supported 'corporate underwriting' (what others regarded as 'advertising', but which she took to be 'sponsorship'), she was insistent that the ABC could not be run like a business, as such a model is as incompatible with the institutional nature of a public broadcaster as it is with that of a university.

What defined her tenure as chairman, however, was her handling of conflict with the Hawke Government in the last five months of the Commission's life. She maintained she had upheld the ABC's independence; the government, that she had failed to act without fear or favour. The dispute centred on complaints Bob Hawke made about radio programmes at the beginning of the election campaign and then a Four Corners television programme.

On 3 February 1983, Fraser called a federal election and

Hawke replaced Bill Hayden as leader of the opposition. Shortly after the election campaign commenced, ABC Radio's AM programme broadcast an interview with the prime minister in which an ABC staff member made a quip at Fraser's expense, for which she was subsequently reprimanded by a member of the ABC management (who was alleged by Hawke to 'have ties' with the Liberal Party). On another occasion, a member of the ABC staff said on the AM programme that Hawke had been mentioned in the secret volume of the Costigan Royal Commission report, implying that he was involved in tax evasion, a claim that Hawke regarded as defamatory. Hawke placed a telephone call to Kramer and told her that he had Senator John Button on the line with him. He said that he believed the ABC was not acting impartially, and insisted that Kramer take action to restore impartiality. Kramer's response was to point out that such decisions are for management, and that she was a non-executive chairman, so she would make enquiries with management. She made enquiries with management and was satisfied that management had acted within their authority. She maintained that it was neither for her to condone nor not to condone the management decision, but simply to satisfy herself that, whether or not it was a good decision, it was a decision within the authority of the person who made it. She communicated this to Button, but he remained convinced that the chairman was condoning the management decisions.

The second incident involved 'The Big League', a report that aired on the Four Corners television programme on 30 April 1983. The programme was concerned with the activities of Rugby League, and in particular the circumstances in which nine counts of fraud against

Kevin Humphreys, the chairman of New South Wales and Australia Rugby League, were dismissed by Kevin Jones, the magistrate before whom he appeared. It was alleged that the Chief Stipendiary Magistrate, Murray Farquhar, had attempted to influence the committal proceedings before Humphreys, and that Farquhar had acted at the direction or request of the Premier of New South Wales, Neville Wran.

Kramer maintained that she was briefed about the report on 29 April, but that this was *for information* rather than *for approval*. She took the view that the decision to air the programme was a decision for management. The decision having been made; she vigorously defended the management decision. Button took the view that the chairman was in a position to prevent the programme from being broadcast and her failure to do so demonstrated that she was not genuinely independent. Wran brought proceedings for defamation immediately, but subsequently dropped them. He also established a royal commission led by the Chief Justice of New South Wales, Sir Laurence Street, which found that Farquhar had influenced the proceedings, but was not acting at the direction or request of Wran.

Button used parliamentary privilege to make an attack on Kramer, claiming that she had not always acted without fear or favour. He saw a parallel between her conduct in relation to the radio incidents during the election campaign and the Four Corners decision that raised allegations about a Labor premier. He was convinced that this demonstrated that Kramer was not impartial and was condoning comments detrimental to the interests of Labor Party politicians.

Richard Carlton interviewed Kramer and Button together on ABC's television programme, Nationwide, shortly after Button's attack on Kramer in the Senate. It was extremely heated and was further aggravated by technical problems that prevented Button from joining the interview on time. In the interview, Button clearly seeks to score political points by arguing that Kramer has failed to act impartially, and that her Four Corners decision was consistent with her approach to the radio decisions. Kramer gives an impressive performance on the programme. What is impressive is not so much her composure—impressive as this is—she seems perfectly at ease in the cut-and-thrust of politics. Rather, it is her characteristically philosophical approach. She tells Carlton in her opening remarks that everything hinges on one's understanding of 'independence'. She is very clear that part of independence is the principle that the Commission does not interfere in management matters. Her view is that although she *supported* management, that did not mean that she *condoned* management's judgement. She maintains that as non-executive chairman, it was not her role to tell management what to do. When defending management, she maintains it was her duty to support management's authority—providing she was satisfied that it did not exceed its authority. Independence here means that the Commission should ensure there is no interference with management's exercise of its proper authority. Button's response: "I don't intend to play verbal tootsies tonight..."

The Australian Broadcasting Commission came to an end on 30 June 1983 and was replaced by the Australian Broadcasting Corporation. Neither Kramer nor any of commissioners were invited to become directors of the successor corporation. She maintained that this was a result of the Commission's defence of 'The Big League'. Whilst she remained proud of her role in defending the public broadcaster, she was also critical of it at times. In particular, she argued that its coverage of the Gulf War in 1992 was arrogant, ignorant, and in breach of its obligation to parliament and its audience. She believed that its concerns that broadcasting messages of support to Australian sailors serving in the Gulf would jeopardise its independence were "nonsense" as the government's decision had been supported by the opposition.

Her confidence in tackling the Labor Government no doubt influenced those in the Liberal Party who believed that she would have made a good candidate for the Liberal/National ticket for the Senate. John Howard recalls that in the mid-1980s it was talked about, and that, although he was not directly involved, he would have supported her as a candidate. It never progressed beyond conversations to anything more serious, perhaps partly because she lacked the political ambition that others had for her. She was interested in politics and in influencing political discourse without herself having political ambition.

Australians for Constitutional Monarchy

The Australia-Britain Society was established in 1971 as an apolitical and non-commercial friendship society to promote historic links between the two countries. Kramer served as its national president from 1984 until 1993. She was a natural fit for this position, given the value she attached to the relationship between the two countries and their shared tradition.

We have seen that 1945 and 1988-89 were momentous years in Kramer's life, but 1991 was also a year of great significance in her life. It was in that year that the Cold War is often thought to have ended with the dissolution of the Soviet Union, following on from the fall of the Berlin Wall in 1989. In Australia, Paul Keating challenged Bob Hawke for the leadership of the Australian Labor Party—unsuccessfully in June, but then successfully a second time in December, to become Australia's twenty-fourth prime minister. And amidst these national and international developments, the Australian Republican Movement was founded.

The following year was the Queen's *annus horribilis*, when the Prince and Princess of Wales and the Duke and Duchess of York both announced their separations amid great scandal, the Princess Royal divorced her first husband, and fire swept through the state rooms of Windsor Castle. More happily, it was also the year that Australians for Constitutional Monarchy was formed. Michael Kirby (President of the New South Wales Court of Appeal) and Lloyd Waddy QC established the civil society organisation with Tony Abbott (when he finished up as press secretary to the opposition leader, John Hewson) as executive director. It was to be the public voice for those who supported the retention of the current constitutional arrangements, and its foundation council included prominent figures from all sections of society, with a view to demonstrating the breadth of support the status quo enjoyed. Given her presidency of the Australia-

Britain Society, it was natural that Kramer should be counted amongst those selected to represent the different interests that supported the constitutional monarchy—a key institution in the shared tradition.

In 1993, Keating established the Republic Advisory Committee, chaired by Malcolm Turnbull, to advise on the terms on which Australia might become a republic. This was the first step towards the referendum held in 1999. The Australian Republican Movement and Australians for Constitutional Monarchy were the most prominent civil society voices in the debate between 1993 and 1999.

John Howard replaced Alexander Downer as opposition leader in 1995. Downer had mooted the idea of a constitutional convention, along the lines of those held in the 1890s to debate the question of federation, to resolve the issue of whether a referendum should be held on the question of becoming a republic, and, if so, the terms on which the Constitution would be amended. Howard committed to convene such a constitutional convention after the next federal election, if the opposition won the election. Howard won a landslide victory in the federal election in 1996 and became the twenty-fifth prime minister. He honoured his election commitment and convened a constitutional convention. Half the delegates to the convention were elected through a non-compulsory postal ballot. The other half of the delegates were appointed by the prime minister. The appointed delegates were intended to reflect the views of different sections of society. Kramer was one of the appointed delegates. Unsurprisingly, she chose to align herself with the Australians for Constitutional Monarchy delegation.

Kramer addressed the convention on 4 February 1998. Her speech was erudite. It consisted of an analysis of two concepts that the republicans constantly pedalled: 'inevitability' and 'symbolism'. She rejects the idea that it is *inevitable* that Australia will become a republic. Her criticism is not that she thinks it is unlikely to happen, but that historical processes, such as constitutional change, are never inevitable: "What we are saying if we adopt this notion is that we, citizens of a stable and advanced democracy, are powerless in the face of the forces of change. To say this is to treat a deliberate campaign to change our political system as though it were like the cycle of the seasons or the inevitable passage from birth to childhood to maturity, age and death—those natural forces over which we in fact do have no control." Her point is that there is nothing inevitable about constitutional change in a democratic polity. It is always subject to the will of the people, and they are always in a position to accept or reject such change. And there was good reason, she maintained, for sensible people to be cautious about accepting such change: "we have heard repeated claims from the republican side that the Australian people want a republic in the absence of any solid evidence, thereby implying both that they, the republicans, know the will of the people and that they have a special entitlement to tell us how things should be in the future of our country. On the other hand, we, the opposition, are concerned about the people who are not delegates to this Convention and who recognise the benefits of our existing Constitution and who do not want to be propelled into an uncertain future." She concluded this section of her remarks by observing that "Inevitability suggests an omniscience which I do not have and you do not have, and none of us have... As Keynes said, the inevitable never happens; what happens is the unpredictable."

When she turned to symbolism, she queried what precisely is necessary in order to achieve the kind of 'symbolic' change that the republicans craved: "Some of the resentment expressed by republicans against the system focuses on matters which it is entirely in our power to change—and they know that very well and I do not know why they do not concede it. For example, a great fuss was made and repeated today about the toast to the Queen at public functions such as the visit of President Clinton. The Prime Minister set another example this week by toasting Australia. We could also if we wished toast the Governor-General. In this, as in other matters, we have a free choice and are not bound, as the republicans seem to imagine, by irrelevant archaisms." Her point is that if what is desired is new symbols, these can be created without substantive change to the Constitution, so it is misleading to suggest that the only way to address Australian symbolism is through constitutional change.

Much of the speech can be understood as a critique of the reformers' agenda, and why they present it in a (deliberately) misleading way. Kramer was confident when it came to offering such criticism of her opponents. She was less inclined to speak in her own voice, however, when it came to explaining the inherent value of preserving the monarchy as part of the shared tradition that she sought to foster as president of the Australia-Britain Society. In order to do this, she chose to end her speech by quoting from the speech delivered by George Mye on the first day of the convention:

"I would like to quote what I think is a very moving and very significant passage which all of us who think of ourselves as Australians should take truly to heart. After talking about the 'Coming of the Light' to the Torres Strait region, he said: 'The Queen became the head of our church and central to the religious, cultural and civic traditions of the people of the Torres Strait. To this day, this remains at the centre of our cultural life in the Torres Strait. By removing the Queen, we remove a way of teaching that has been passed on to our children over many generations. The monarchy is an essential element of our history and cultural inheritance. Its removal will deeply affect the fabric of our society.' I want to thank Mr Mye in his presence for that statement and remind republicans that, if they take on this grave responsibility, they may indeed have a lot to answer for."

She was less circumspect when the convention was debating what matters should be mentioned in the preamble to a republican constitution, interjecting, "I simply want to remark that this is very far from being a preamble. It is more like a compendium or a wish list. I know it is too late for me to say this, in a sense, but I want to register the view that the whole philosophy behind this is mistaken."

Howard introduced a Bill for a Constitution Alteration to remove the role of the Queen and the Governor-General from the Constitution and to replace them with a president elected by a special majority of the Parliament, as recommended in the communique from the Constitutional Convention. The Bill was passed by both Houses of

Parliament and a referendum was held in November 1999, as required by section 128 of the Constitution. In a break with the practice for previous referendum campaigns, Howard decided that $7,500,000 of public funds would be allocated to an official Yes Case campaign committee and to an official No Case campaign committee, the members of each being selected by the prime minister. Each committee would then devise a campaign to promote their best case and would be able to use the public funds to publicise it.

Kramer was invited to sit on the No Case committee, along with other monarchists and republicans opposed to the specific model for a republic. The No Case committee published a volume containing eighteen papers by different authors. Kramer wrote a five-sentence foreword to the collection, and those sentences disclose a lot about her approach to the campaign. She wrote of the need for "deep consideration" about "the best way to preserve our democracy" and the need to "promote Australia's future prosperity through continuing political stability." She explains that the contributors, though differing in many respects, "agree that it is vital not to be rushed headlong into major political changes, the alleged advantages of which their proponents are not able or willing to define." To vote against this republic "is not to obstruct Australia's progress, or to endanger our valuable relationships with other countries" but to "demonstrate our faith in the constitution." At the subsequent referendum, her side prevailed and the proponents of change were defeated.

Feminism

Kramer was known for her opposition to feminism, yet she devotes a mere four pages to the subject under the heading, 'Secret Women's Business' in her memoirs, *Broomstick*. Surprisingly, she begins by referring to "Biblical matters" and her recollections of attending chapel as a student. From there, she moves on to the feminists' preoccupation with power and their calls for empowerment. This leads on to a brief discussion of "the rewards of domesticity", before offering some reflections on her observations of student life at Oxford. She then provides an anecdote from an encounter after she returned to Australia in the 1950s which seems to capture the nature of the predicament she faced: "A neighbour summed it up by asking me, 'When is your husband going to be able to keep you properly?'" Finally, she returns to her objection to radical feminists and concludes, "I am unsympathetic with those feminists (or for that matter, anyone else) who are in a hurry to change the world in their favour."

In 1995, Kramer attracted attention for her comments on women's purported experience of discrimination in the workplace as part of a wider-ranging interview. She told her local newspaper, the *Sydney Weekly*, that some women in academia disadvantaged themselves by "talking too much" and "actually trading on their femininity." This remark was picked up by the broadsheets, and the *Sydney Morning Herald* ran a frontpage story on 23 June under the headline, "Women go limp when going gets tough: Kramer." It was explained that although Kramer was one of a very small group of women who had made it to professorial rank, she did not believe that women's failure to achieve this rank had anything to do with discrimination against women. She attributed the failure of women to reach the top tier to their lack of self-confidence and qualifications. Although she acknowledged that she had faced obstacles in her career, she maintained they "were not placed there because I am a woman." Some women, she surmised, were content to get near the top without taking the final step; others chose to abandon their academic careers to "go off and do something else."

What are we to make of these remarks? Kramer was one of the first women to reach the upper echelons of the academy. Writing in *Broomstick*, she explains, "I consciously discarded the all-absorbing life of a full-time scholar in favour of domesticity." She does not regret the choice that she made and writes glowingly of the rewards of domesticity. The suggestion is that she was not particularly career ambitious. This is consistent with the way that she explains her roles in public life: she suggests that she did not seek them out, but rather that people approached her. There is a sense that the course her life took was unplanned and lacked personal ambition—or at least that that is her own understanding of it. Her detractors will say that she had the benefit of a wealthy and supportive husband who enabled her to pursue her career whilst at the same time managing a household.

Intellectually formidable she undoubtedly was, and her academic success can be traced to this. There is also a sense, however, that she was the right man at the right time. In an era in which corporate boards were starting to realise that it was appropriate and even advantageous for them to have a woman on their board, they saw in Kramer a no-

nonsense and pragmatic woman with whom they could do business. So it was her personal attributes as much as her intellectual capacity and her supportive husband that enabled her to achieve.

Her comments at the close of the twentieth century need to be seen in the context of having been made by someone who was a pioneer half a century earlier. It may seem ridiculous to career-focused women now, but Kramer seems to have genuinely felt that the prejudice she faced in the 1950s was the prejudice of other women who thought that, as a woman, her place was to be the homemaker not the breadwinner. Given that there is now wide acceptance that it should be possible to be both a homemaker and a breadwinner, the question is now whether the conditions exist that enable ordinary women to be both breadwinners and homemakers.

A quarter of a century after her 1995 remarks, it seems clear that the position of women in the workplace has not improved as much as she might have anticipated. Speaking on International Women's Day in 2021, the prime minister, Scott Morrison, acknowledged "that girls and women deserve an equal stake in our economy and our society" but that "we still have a long way to go" in achieving this. Kramer may well have been correct that ideological responses proposed by the feminists would not solve the problem. That is not to say, however, that they did not identify a real problem. It is central to Kramer's Burkean outlook that social problems are not solved by having recourse to theory. She rejects the feminists' Foucauldian analysis of society in terms of power and their agenda for empowering women. She would say that the right response to the problem is gradual change of a practical nature, through which traditional institutions adapt to changing social circumstances. That might be the right approach, but in too many areas such change has not occurred effectively enough since 1995, suggesting that the glass ceiling that she denied existed may still be in place.

Miles Franklin Prize and the Demidenko affair

In 1993, Helen Demidenko was awarded The Australian/Vogel Literary Award. In 1994, her manuscript was published by Allen & Unwin under the title, *The Hand that Signed the Paper*. In 1995, the novel won the Miles Franklin Literary Prize and the Australian Literary Society Gold Medal. In between the announcement of the prize and the gold medal, Demidenko was unmasked as Helen Darville, a young woman of English ancestry, who had been masquerading as the daughter of Ukrainian and Irish immigrants in the most spectacular literary hoax in Australia since the Ern Malley affair.

The novel begins in Australia in the early 1990s, when a young woman discovers that family members who immigrated to Australia from the Ukraine had been complicit in atrocities committed by the Nazis during the German occupation of the Ukraine during the Second World War, and, in particular, the notorious massacre of more than 33,000 Jews at Babi Yar in 1941. What is revealed is that these ethnic Ukrainian characters felt justified in participating in the massacres because they believed that the atrocities visited upon ethnic Ukrainians under Communist rule were the work of ethnic Jews. On one reading of it, this is a story about man's inhumanity to man. On another reading, however, the novel seems to be saying that the Ukrainians' antisemitism and participation in acts of genocide were justified because of their beliefs about Jewish support for the Stalinist regime that oppressed the Ukrainians. On the latter reading, the novel seems to vindicate Ukrainian antisemitism.

The literary qualities of the novel have been debated at some length. That it was worthy of the Vogel is, perhaps, less contentious, as this is awarded for unpublished manuscripts by writers under the age of thirty-five. Thus, it is to be expected that the quality of the manuscript might be uneven and in need of further editing before it is ready to be published. The Australian Literary Society Gold Medal is awarded annually for an outstanding literary work in the preceding calendar year, and so the bar for the gold medal is set somewhat higher than that for the Vogel. When the medal was awarded in 1995, the literary hoax had already been revealed, and so the award was made in full knowledge of this. The Miles Franklin Literary Prize is awarded for a novel which is of the highest literary merit and presents Australian life in any of its phases. This is the most prestigious of the three literary awards. In 1995, it was awarded before the hoax was exposed.

The Miles Franklin Prize was first awarded in 1957 to Patrick White for *Voss*. Kramer had been a member of the judging committee since 1984, and served as its chairman until 1997. In 1995, the other members of the committee were H. P. Heseltine, Adrian Mitchell, and Jill Kitson. It was Kramer, as chairman, who was the focus of much of the criticism, together with Kitson, who had previously championed Demidenko. In the face of criticism, the judges were reticent to speak to the press about the literary and other values that informed their decision. Kitson, was the exception, however, explaining that the expression of antisemitism in the novel was not "one of the things that concerned our discussions. We were much more concerned about literary qualities." When Kramer first discussed the matter on 29 August 1995, she said, "I am puzzled by the rage of some commentators" and that this "sustained and vitriolic attack on the book and its author . . . calls into question our claims to be a tolerant and fair-minded society."

Since winning the Vogel, Demidenko had paraded around the speaking circuit in traditional Ukrainian peasant attire, rejoicing in folk dance and drinking vodka. She took every opportunity to drop Ukrainian words into her speeches and to present as a proud ethnic Ukrainian who had grown up in Australia. So the accusation that she had been selected as the committee's 'token' ethnic winner—its concession to multiculturalism—quickly surfaced. Here, after all, was a book in which a young Ukrainian Australian reflected on the legacy of her Ukrainian ancestry. When the Ukrainian Demidenko was subsequently unmasked as the English Darville, it was a great source of mirth that, in having compromised its commitment to recognising the highest literary merit for the sake of appearing to embrace 'ethnics', the committee had been duped and had rewarded a faux-ethnic for a novel that lacked the highest literary merit.

Aside from objections on the grounds that the novel lacked the highest literary merit, there were objections of a more legalistic nature, namely that the novel, which is primarily set outside Australia, did not meet the requirement set out in the terms of the bequest that the novel must present Australian life in any of its phases. The committee might have claimed some wriggle room on this point but for the fact that the previous year several books had been deemed ineligible because they did not sufficiently engage with Australian life. Given the previous year's determination, it was hardly surprising that detractors objected to the choice of a book that is primarily concerned with conflicts between Ukrainians, Jews, Germans, and Russians in Eastern Europe.

Literary and legal considerations aside, the decision to make the award to Demidenko caused commentators to question it on the basis of broader cultural and moral concerns. The novel does not condemn Ukrainian antisemitism—it simply acknowledges it as an historical fact. At best, it is silent about the morality of Ukrainian antisemitism; at worst, it offers a justification for it. It is hardly surprising that leaders of the Jewish community actively condemned the novel as antisemitic. These accusations met with counterclaims from the Ukrainian community in Australia.

The accusation was not merely that Demidenko/Darville had written an antisemitic work. It was that the pre-eminent literary prize had been given to an antisemitic work. Not only that, it was a prize for a novel that presented Australian life in any of its phases. So, if it could be awarded to a work that depicted antisemitism without condemning it, this suggested that antisemitism was to be recognised as one of the phases of Australian life; and a phase of Australian life that could be recognised without passing adverse moral judgment.

In 1996, Andrew Riemer wrote a book about the affair, entitled *The Demidenko Debate*. Later in the same year, Robert Manne published *The Culture of Forgetting*, which offers an alternative perspective. He writes, "Where Andrew Riemer appears to see in Australia's ability to publish and honour a book like *The Hand* evidence of a culture so at ease with itself that it is unfussed even by a tolerably antisemitic novel about the Holocaust, I see in it, rather, evidence of historical amnesia and of a culture which, on this occasion, has run adrift from its moorings." Alas, it is not possible to consider in detail these two competing interpretations at present. Rather, we must focus on Kramer's role in it.

The Riemer approach supports Kramer's concern that the novel's detractors were threatening the foundations of Australia as a free society; what she seemed to think constituted a cultural *fatwa*. This seems to be unjustified. There was almost no attempt to silence Demidenko through recourse to anti-discrimination law. Hardly anyone said the book should be censored or that a publisher should not have been permitted to publish it. Rather, the concern was that a publisher chose to publish it and that it received the highest literary accolades in Australia. Kramer seemed unwilling to accept that those who were upset felt this way because the custodians of Australian high culture saw value in a literary work that seemed to trivialise the significance of the Holocaust.

Kitson claimed that the Miles Franklin judges were only concerned with literary qualities. It is an open question whether the novel was ethically flawed on account of its treatment of Ukrainian antisemitism, and, if so, whether this constituted a literary flaw. The difficulty remains, however, that she and Kramer did not seem to see the need to address other readers' concerns about the non-literary qualities. Kramer either did not appreciate or did not want to validate the concerns of those who thought the treatment of the Holocaust was morally problematic. This is all the more curious in a woman whose husband, and possibly her children, would have fallen foul of the Nuremberg Laws. A better response would have been to acknowledge the legitimacy of these concerns before explaining why they were not relevant to an assessment of the novel's literary qualities. In a fair-minded society, there might be legitimate disagreement about whether the novel's treatment of the Holocaust affected its literary qualities, but there would also need to be an acknowledgement of the morally problematic nature of this treatment of the Holocaust at the outset of the debate.

Kramer was very keen to rebuff the suggestion that the prize had been awarded to a 'token ethnic'. When the hoax was exposed, she was not particularly fussed about it. These stances are understandable. One can even understand her determination that the prize should not be concerned with non-literary qualities of a novel. What is more difficult to justify, however, is her tone deafness to the non-literary objections; her refusal to engage with them, even if only to explain why, though legitimate moral objections, they were not relevant to the judges' decision.

Quadrant and Robert Manne

In 1956, *Quadrant* published its first magazine. It was founded by Richard Krygier with James McAuley as its first editor. The magazine was a product of the Cold War and was published under the aegis of the Australian Committee for Cultural Freedom, which was the local arm of the Congress for Cultural Freedom (which the CIA was subsequently revealed to have helped establish and fund). It was an unashamedly anti-communist voice in Australian cultural life.

As it happens, 1956 was also the year that Harry and Leonie Kramer moved their family from Canberra to Sydney. Leonie did not yet have an academic post in Sydney, and McAuley recruited her to assist with the editorial work for *Quadrant*. In this way, Kramer had been involved with the magazine from its inception, and her rise to prominence paralleled that of the magazine. She accepted the chairmanship of its board of directors in 1986, at a time when she had established a reputation as one of Australia's most formidable conservative public intellectuals, and she remained its chairman until 1999. This period overlapped with Robert Manne's editorship (1990-1997). McAuley had edited the magazine throughout its first decade, and then Peter Coleman edited it for two decades (which were bookended by Donald Horne and Roger Sandall's brief editorships). Manne's seven-year stint ended in 1997, when he was succeeded by P. P. McGuiness for the next decade. Since then, Keith Windschuttle has served as editor, save for two years when John O'Sullivan filled the post.

Manne's time as editor was a notable period in the history of the magazine. The circulation increased considerably, and a wider range of contributors wrote for it. It was also a fraught period, however, when ideological disagreement became difficult to contain, and ultimately led to Manne's departure. Having taken over in 1990, Manne first offered his resignation in 1992. This was not accepted by the board. A compromise was reached and Kramer issued a statement in the October issue of *Quadrant* to this effect. This was followed by a statement of the magazine's 'deep values'; a statement which was intended, one assumes, to provide an intellectual basis on which Manne could work alongside those who disagreed increasingly profoundly with him. Manne offered his resignation for a second time in 1997, when it was accepted and McGuiness was appointed as the new editor. Manne's tenure saw the magazine's readership increase and a wider range of contributors write for it, but it had also called into question what the magazine stood for. The tensions can be traced to competing attitudes to neoliberalism, the Demidenko affair, the claim that Manning Clark received the Order of Lenin, and finally the 'Stolen Generations'.

With the end of the Cold War, the common cause shared by those on the board of *Quadrant* started to break up. Kramer was seen to be closely aligned with Hugh Morgan, the CEO of Western Mining, who was a driving force behind neoliberalism or the New Right in Australian commercial life and public discourse. Neoliberalism is a broadly libertarian approach to politics which is primarily centred on free market economics and capitalism. An influential neoliberal industrial relations think-tank at this time was the HR Nichols Society, which was driven by Ray Evans, Morgan's executive officer, and the arguments of Evans and Morgan were very much at home in *Quadrant*.

In contrast, however, Manne was increasingly interested in offering a critique of neoliberalism—including in the pages of *Quadrant*.

The economic disagreements were then joined by cultural disagreements. Manne became one of the most prominent critics of *The Hand that Signed the Paper* and of the critical acclaim that it received. This was bound to be a source of tension, given that Kramer chaired the judging panel that awarded the prize as well as serving as chairman of the magazine Manne edited.

The third dimension was of a more personal nature. In 1996, it was alleged in the *Courier-Mail* that the iconic Australian historian, Manning Clark, had been awarded the Order of Lenin. A Press Council investigation concluded that the newspaper did not have adequate evidence for the allegations and should not have published them. *Quadrant*'s literary editor was the celebrated poet, Les Murray. Murray believed the allegations were correct and became obsessed with Manne's rejection of the allegations. Manne found Murray's editorial decisions unacceptable and the tone of his communications personally offensive to the point that he resolved to remove Murray as literary editor of the magazine. According to his account, Kramer as chairman initially backed Manne in this matter, but then reneged: "Kramer misled me with an elegant insouciance I could almost admire." Her reversal was critical to Manne's decision to resign as editor.

The most serious rift was, however, over attitudes to the treatment of Aboriginal people in Australian history, in particular as this was presented in the Australian Human Rights Commission's *Bringing Them Home* report on the removal of Aboriginal and Torres Strait Islander children from their families (who came to be known as the 'Stolen Generations'). The report found that forcible removal of children had been the policy of various governments across Australia and recommended that reparations should be paid to those who were affected and that the various Australian legislatures should acknowledge the responsibility of their predecessors and offer apologies for these policies. This report prompted Manne to reflect on his own understanding of Australian history, and he used the pages of *Quadrant* to articulate his developing insights, which were broadly of a piece with the approach taken in the report. In contrast, a number of members of the magazine's board took serious exception to the report. As such, they were not willing for *Quadrant* to become a vehicle for the new approach to Australian history. Manne was not prepared to continue editing a magazine whose board was at best divided about, at worst opposed to, his take on the history of Aboriginal experiences since 1788. For him, this was as much a moral dispute as it was an intellectual dispute.

Two opposing analyses of Kramer's involvement in Manne's decision to resign suggest themselves. To her detractors, Kramer was a crony of Hugh Morgan (on whose board she sat at Western Mining). Martin Krygier, son of *Quadrant*'s founder, was on the magazine's board at the time. He saw in Kramer's approach to neoliberalism evidence of what he calls the 'hunting in packs' that plagues intellectual life in Australia—the sense in which factions band together to support one another's stances, so that thoughtful and respectful disagreement becomes impossible. On this reading, *Quadrant* was the home patch of neoliberalism, and there was no room for those who might start to offer a critique of it. In terms of the Demidenko affair, she seemed to her detractors to be the embodiment of the patricians' blindness to antisemitism in Australia. As for the growing rift between Manne and Murray, she seemed at best aloof or indifferent. When it came to the Stolen Generations, she seemed to be part of a reactionary cabal that was incapable of engaging with the hard truths about Australian history.

Viewed from another perspective, her stance on some, if not all, of these matters might seem more moderate. In terms of neoliberalism, she claimed not to hold particularly strong views. Although he observed a "New Right bulletin on her university desk" when he interviewed her, Craig McGregor reports that she disclaimed it, saying, "I'm not a member of the H. R. Nicholls Society, I don't even know who H. R. Nicholls was. I'm a terrible dumbhead about this; I have no idea what the New Right is, who they are; I can't stand labels or slogans, all those things that try to make it simple for you not to think. I believe in private enterprise but I'm not an absolute free market forces person; I don't believe in the Moral Majority. I'm not an extremist." There is probably something to Krygier's assessment, however, as Kramer was probably given to supporting the stronger views of those around her whom she trusted in such matters. Even if she did not explicitly adopt them as her own, she would have implicitly sanctioned them.

As for the seeming indifference about the escalating dispute between Murray and Manne over the Order of Lenin, a predilection towards a disinterested stance was a matter of Kramer's personal style. It was probably also true, however, that managing such interpersonal tensions was not her forte. Her strength was as a strenuous advocate for an intellectually unpopular position, not in reconciling those in conflict. This would not be particularly helpful for a chairman trying to resolve conflict.

In terms of the Demidenko affair, her stance needs to be understood in terms of her determination that decisions about a novel must be made through the prism of literary merit, not through the prism of its broader cultural significance. As such, she was entitled to her assessment of the relevance of the novel's antisemitism for its literary merit, and other literary critics may disagree with this assessment. The difficulty is not so much that she was blind to (what she regarded as) the non-literary significance of antisemitism, but that she did not see the need to engage with it. She had a tendency to identify a narrow issue that was relevant to the resolution of a broader problem, and then insist that this was the only relevant consideration. This was as true when it came to her work in Australian literature as it was when discussing proposals for constitutional change. She may well have identified the critical issue in each case. The difficulty is that her approach was then to disregard other considerations, rather than to demonstrate an understanding of them before explaining why they were not relevant to the proper resolution of the dispute.

Finally, there is her approach to the Stolen Generations. There is no way around the fact that she, as chairman, led the group on the *Quadrant* board that opposed Manne's stance. Her approach to this issue probably combined aspects of her approach to neoliberalism, the Manne-

Murray dispute, and the Demidenko affair, but there is also something uncharitable and combative about an assessment of her as an unqualified reactionary on this issue. At the Constitutional Convention, she rose to speak in a debate about the preamble to a republican constitution. She said, "Everyone here by now knows I am anti-republican, but we all agreed that the Commonwealth of Australia should be the name of a republic, should there be one. I want to appeal for you all to agree unanimously, as we did the other day, to the inclusion of Aboriginal people and Torres Strait Islanders in the preamble." The form of constitutional recognition that was proposed in 1998 falls significantly short of the form of constitutional recognition that was called for by Indigenous people in the 2017 Uluru Statement from the Heart. What seemed like a consensus position then, was far from a consensus position thirty years later, and we cannot know what her stance would have been in 2017. What is significant is that, in the midst of intense dispute about other matters, she could see that certain aspects of this issue had moved beyond partisanship.

That the resignations of Manne in 1997 and Kramer in 2001 were petty victories for opposing sides in Australia's culture wars can be a source of little consolation for anyone.

6
A woman for all seasons

When she died in 2016, the *Sydney Morning Herald* ran an obituary that opened with the following sentence: "A formidable educator who extolled old-fashioned virtues, Leonie Kramer was a traditionalist who, ironically, came to personify a changing order."

There is no doubt that she had a commitment to values that some might regard as 'old-fashioned' and also that her life personified a changing order. We would do well, however, to consider what the newspaper regards as so ironical about this. The irony waxes when one appreciates that the obituarists maintain that the deceased can be summed up as a 'traditionalist'; one who demonstrates excessive respect for traditional ways of doing things. There is, indeed, something ironical about such a traditionalist personifying a changing order.

Kramer was someone deeply committed to tradition, but that does not necessarily make her a traditionalist. She was not wedded to the traditional way of doing things. Had she been, she would have criticised the prime minister for taking liberties with the loyal toast; she would have insisted that he should have used the traditional toasting formula, "Gentlemen, the Queen." That she praised, rather than berated him, demonstrates the sense in which she believed in tradition without being a traditionalist. She saw that things had to change; that change was not in and of itself a bad thing; that tradition is not static; and that those conservatives who are committed to tradition embrace change in conformity with tradition.

Rather than 'traditionalist', Kramer preferred to adopt Sir Keith Hancock's phrase, 'radical conservative', to describe herself. She told Richard Coleman in an interview for the *Sydney Morning Herald* in 1982 that this captures both her commitment to traditional values and the necessity of reforming institutions, although she was aware of the difficulty that this seemed to present: "One thing I find hard to explain is my sense of a necessary connection between a regard for traditional values and change. Because you can't preserve interest in the past simply by trying to hold on to it." To say that her life embodied a changing order is to say that her life exemplified the way in which she believed Australian culture, society, and government could and should change in conformity with tradition. When seen in this light, the sense of irony wanes.

That this might not have been understood by her obituarists would not have surprised her. As she told Coleman, "Over the years I have become resigned to being misrepresented. I sometimes think is it never possible to make oneself clear?" Perhaps, she did not see the need to explain her deepest intuitions or the reasons why she had made certain career choices. She seemed to be aware of both the coherence and the incoherence in what she had done, and she was at peace with that, explaining to Coleman, "I believe in the absolute importance of excellence in every area of life. It's hard to see my activities as systematic or co-ordinated but in all of them I have tried to make a reasonably consistent contribution. I have tried to get things right and I have tried to get as deep an understanding as I can in the various areas in which I have worked. And I have always done my homework."

Having noted that "during a spectacular working life,

Kramer achieved fame as a critic, editor, administrator, scholar and uncompromising controversialist," the *Herald*'s obituarists then write that "she emerged as a woman for all seasons, applying her abundant energies to the world of business and public sector organisations." This gloss does little to impose coherence on her life, but it reveals more than the opening attempt at irony.

To say that Kramer was a woman for all seasons is to allude to the title of Robert Bolt's 1954 BBC radio play (which was subsequently reworked for a West End theatrical production) about the life of Sir Thomas More, *A Man for All Seasons*. The title itself is an allusion to Robert Whittington's remark in his *Vulgaria* (1520) that "Moore is a man of an aungels wyt / & syngler lernyng. He is a man of many excellent vertues (yf I shold say as it is) I knowe not his felowe. For where is the man (in whome is so many goodly vertues) of y^t gentylnes / lowlynes / and affabylyte. And as tyme requyreth / a man of merveylous myrth and pastymes / & somtyme of as sad gravyte / as who say. a man for all seasons." It brings to mind Michael Kirby's reminiscence of his time working with Kramer in defence of the constitutional monarchy in the 1990s: "Leonie Kramer was a voice of rationalism . . . she abhorred arguments of envy, of old enmities and emotional nationalism . . . She was always cool and self-possessed. She never descended to personal vituperation . . . She kept an historical perspective. She also kept her sense of humour. Working in the same cause with Leonie Kramer is fun . . . She was boundless in her energy to promote a true debate . . . Dame Leonie's commitment to reason, calm persuasion and an honest statement of beliefs cannot be doubted."

This chain from the *Sydney Morning Herald* obituarising

Kramer in 2016, back through Bolt's play title in 1954 to Whittington's comment in 1520 exemplifies the sense of tradition that Kramer valued, and which makes sense of the way in which her life personified change. As an undergraduate at the University of Melbourne, she read the work of R. G. Collingwood, the Waynflete Professor of Metaphysical Philosophy at Oxford, who died shortly before the Second World War. In his *Roman Britain and the English Settlements*, Collingwood writes, "The continuity of tradition is the continuity of the force by which past experiences affect the future: and this force does not depend on the conscious memory of those experiences. In the life of a people, a great experience in the past affects the way in which the generation that has had it teaches its children to look at the future, even though they never knew what that experience was."

Dame Leonie Kramer understood that the continuity of this force goes beyond the way in which Whittington's way of talking about his contemporary in 1520 influences Bolt's artistic endeavour in 1954, which ultimately influences a newspaper's obituarists in 2016. However much things had changed since Edmund Burke's day, Kramer agreed with Burke that this force was the best guide for cultural, social, political, and constitutional change. Her life's work is testimony to the force that tradition still has; a force still harnessed by radical conservatives—though not by reactionaries any more than revolutionaries—when approaching change.

Sources

The following is not intended to be a comprehensive bibliography, but merely a set of references for readers who wish to follow up the key sources referred to in the text.

Broomstick: Personal Reflections of Leonie Kramer (Australian Scholarly, 2012) offers Kramer's most sustained reflections on her career, although it suffers from the onset of dementia during the final stages of its preparation. Kramer's other publications as author include *Henry Handel Richardson and Some of her Sources* (Melbourne University Press, 1954) published under her maiden name, Leonie J. Gibson; *A Companion to Australia Felix* (Heinemann Australia, 1962); *Myself When Laura: Fact and Fiction in Henry Handel Richardson's School Career* (Heinemann Australia, 1966); *A. D. Hope* (Oxford University Press, 1979). Her publications as editor include *Oxford History of Australian Literature* (Oxford University Press, 1981); *Oxford Anthology of Australian Literature* (Oxford University Press, 1985); *My Country: Australian Poetry and Short Stories—Two Hundred Years*, Vols I and II (Lansdown-Rigby, 1985); *David Campbell: Collected Poems* (Angus & Robertson, 1989); and *James McAuley: Collected Poems* (Harper Collins, 1995).

There are numerous short profile pieces about Kramer, however, five key ones that span her five-decade career are Ronald McKie, "Women Bore Men", *Australian Women's Weekly*, 2 September 1959; Andrew Clark, "Portrait of a powerful Australian woman", *The Bulletin*, 24 April 1979; Richard Coleman, "Leonie Kramer talks to the right people, all the time", *Sydney Morning Herald*, 20 February 1982; Craig McGregor, "Leonie Kramer" in *Headliners* (University of Queensland Press, 1990); and James Cunningham and Damien Murphy, "Obituary: Dame Leonie Kramer a celebrated academic and a potent conservative voice", *Sydney Morning Herald*, 21 April 2016.

Matters of the Mind: Poems, Essays and Interviews in Honour of Leonie Kramer (University of Sydney, 2001), a festschrift edited by Lee Jobling and Catherine Runcie, contains a number of chapters discussing aspects of Kramer's career. Of especial significance are Keith Mackriell's "Beyond the Bounds of Judgment" about Kramer's time as chairman of the ABC; Michael Kirby's "Leonie Kramer and the Constitution" about her involvement with Australians for Constitutional Monarchy; and Harry Heseltine's "Leonie Kramer and Australian Literary Studies: A Personal View".

On Patrick White, see five articles in *Quadrant*: Harry Heseltine's "Patrick White's Style", June 1963; and Kramer's four articles: "Patrick White's Götterdämmerung", June 1973; "Patrick White: 'The Unplayed I'", February 1974; "Pseudoxia Endemica", July 1980; and "Home Thoughts from Abroad", January-February 1982. There are passing references to Kramer in Patrick White's *Flaws in the Glass: a self-portrait* (Penguin, 1981) and David Marr's *Patrick White: A Life* (Vintage, 1991) and his edited collection, *Patrick White: Letters* (Randon House, 1994).

The Oxford History of Australian Literature was extensively reviewed, and for a survey of a number of reviews, see Bruce King, "Review: An Unhistorical History of Australian Literature", *Sewanee Review*, 1982, Vol. 90. The most vigorous criticism is to be found in John Docker's "Leonie Kramer in the Prison House of Criticism", *Overland*, 1982, Vol. 85. For Kramer's response, see her contribution to Richard Freadman (ed.), *Literature, Criticism and the Universities: interviews with Leonie Kramer, S. L. Goldberg and Howard Felperin* (Centre for Studies in Australian Literature, University of Western Australia, 1983).

For Kramer's account of the challenges the education system poses for preserving cultural heritage, see her chapter, "A Heritage for our Children" in James Ramsay (ed.), *Our Heritage and Australia's Future* (Schwartz & Wilkinson, 1991), and for a general introduction to the challenge of progressive education in the 1960s and 1970s, and the role of the Australian Council for Educational Standards, see Graeme Willcox, "An Analysis of the Recent Reform Movement in Education: with special reference to Victorian Secondary Schools in the late Nineteen Sixties", Master of Education thesis, University of Melbourne, 1977.

There was extensive coverage of Kramer's time as chairman of the ABC in the daily broadsheets, but of particular interest is Richard Carlton's interview with Kramer and Senator John Button which aired on the ABC's Nationwide television programme on 6 May 1983.

Hansard for the Constitutional Convention held at Old Parliament House, Canberra, 2-13 February 1998, may be found on the Australian Parliament's website.

Two detailed and contrasting studies of the Demidenko affair are Andrew Riemer's *The Demidenko Debate* (Allen & Unwin, 1996) and Robert Manne's *The Culture of Forgetting: Helen Demidenko and the Holocaust* (Text Publishing Company, 1996).

Robert Manne's account of his resignation as editor of *Quadrant* is provided in "Sorry Business", *The Monthly*, March 2008.

A fuller discussion of my treatment of conservatism and sources for quotes from Burke, Disraeli, Collingwood etc may be found in my *Abbott's Right: the conservative tradition from Menzies to Abbott* (Melbourne University Press, 2017).

Acknowledgments

This is neither a biography of Dame Leonie Kramer AC DBE nor a comprehensive assessment of her scholarship. It is a contribution to the Australian Biographical Monographs series, which seeks to acquaint a wider readership with Professor Kramer as a public figure, and, in doing so, with the continuity between her public and scholarly lives, in the hope that others might be inspired to take on the more onerous tasks of biography and cultural history. As such, it is a deliberately slim volume. Notwithstanding this, it has benefited from many minds who have assisted in its development in a multitude of ways. The foremost contribution is that of my research assistant, Ethan Westwood Esq, who has done a stellar job of helping me get across the range of sources relevant to this project. In addition to published material, I have benefited from the insights of those who knew my subject, including the Hon. J. W. Howard OM AC, the Hon. M. D. Kirby AC CMG, the Hon. A. J. Abbott AC, Emeritus Professor H. P. Heseltine AO, the Hon. L. D. S. Waddy AM RFD QC, Emeritus Professor Elizabeth Webby AM, Professor M. E. J. Krygier AM, J. A. McCarthy Esq QC, Professor Barry Spurr, Professor J. W. Franklin, Dr Susan Moore, J. M. Hyde Esq, and Ms Santina Rizzo. Professor Heseltine, along with my colleague at the PM Glynn Institute, Dr Lukas Opacic, and our director, Dr M. A. Casey, kindly read the manuscript and gave me the benefit of their different perspectives on it. I also owe a special debt to J. A. Berbotto Esq: he paid close attention to the manuscript and proved keen to embrace its author's versatility.

D. T. F.
Australian Catholic University, North Sydney

Also by Damien Freeman

AUTHOR

Roddy's Folly: R. P. Meagher QC—art lover and lawyer

Art's Emotions: Ethics, expression and aesthetic experience

The Aunt's Mirrors: Family experience and meaningfulness—a memoir

Abbott's Right: The conservative tradition from Menzies to Abbott

EDITOR

Mao's Toe
Memoirs of the life of David Chipp—a serious correspondent

Today's Tyrants: Responding to Dyson Heydon

The Market's Morals: Responding to Jesse Norman

Tribalism's Troubles: Responding to Rowan Williams

Faith's Place: Democracy in a religious world
(with Bryan Turner)

Figuring Out Figurative Art
Contemporary philosophers on contemporary paintings
(with Derek Matravers)

The Forgotten People
Liberal and conservative approaches to recognising indigenous peoples
(with Shireen Morris)

Nonsense on Stilts: Rescuing human rights in Australia
(with Catherine Renshaw)

PAMPHLETEER

The Australian Declaration of Recognition
Declaring our national identity by recognising indigenous Australians
(with Julian Leeser)

Amen
A history of prayers in parliament
(with David Corbett)

www.ingramcontent.com/pod-product-compliance
Lightning Source LLC
Chambersburg PA
CBHW071625170426
43195CB00038B/2128